CULINARY MATH

LINDA BLOCKER + JULIA HILL

CULINARY MATH

3RD EDITION

BICENTENNIAL
1807
WILEY
2007
BICENTENNIAL

JOHN WILEY & SONS, INC.

The Culinary Institute of America
President: Dr. Tim Ryan '77
Vice-President, Continuing Education: Mark Erickson '77
Director of Intellectual Property: Nathalie Fischer
Managing Editor: Kate McBride
Editorial Project Manager: Lisa Lahey '00
Production Assistant: Patrick Decker '05

This book is printed on acid-free paper. ∞

Published by John Wiley & Sons, Inc., Hoboken, New Jersey
Published simultaneously in Canada

Cover and interior design by Vertigo Design, NYC
Composition by North Market Street Graphics, Lancaster, PA

Wiley bicentennial logo design by Richard J. Pacifico

For general information on our other products and services or for technical support, please contact our Customer Care Department within the United States at (800) 762-2974, outside the United States at (317) 572-3993 or fax (317) 572-4002.

Wiley also publishes its books in a variety of electronic formats. Some content that appears in print may not be available in electronic books. For more information about Wiley products, visit our web site at www.wiley.com.

Library of Congress Cataloging-in-Publication Data
Blocker, Linda
    Culinary math / Linda Blocker and Julia Hill.—3rd ed.
        p.   cm.
    Includes index.
    ISBN 978-0-470-06821-2 (pbk.)
    1. Cookery—Mathematics.   I. Hill, Julia, 1954–.   II. Title.
    TX652.B5844 2007
    641.5'01'51—dc22
        2007006011

Printed in the United States of America

10 9 8 7 6 5 4 3 2 1

This book is dedicated to:

My husband, Dr. Seth Blocker, and my children, Rachel and Benjamin Blocker
My parents, Arnold and Roslyn Weiss
My grandmother, Freda Weiss
The memory of my grandfather, Robert Weiss, and my grandmother, Jean Friedlander
—LINDA A. BLOCKER

My husband and daughter, John and Keely Campbell
My mother, Elizabeth Willis Hill
—JULIA H. HILL

We would also like to dedicate this book to the students who found success in this math, perhaps for the first time!

Contents

Acknowledgments

We would like to extend our gratitude to the people at The Culinary Institute of America who helped make this project a reality:

MARK ERICKSON

NATHALIE FISCHER

KATE MCBRIDE

LISA LAHEY

MARY DONOVAN

SUSAN WYSOCKI

BONNIE BOGUSH

LAURA DREESEN

ANTHONY LIGOURI

EZRA EICHELBERGER

We would also like to thank those at John Wiley & Sons for their assistance:

NATALIE CHAPMAN

PAM CHIRLS

CHRISTINE DICOMO

CHRISTINA SOLAZZO

AVA WILDER

And we would also like to thank:

JOHN STORM

MARY COWELL

CATHY POWERS

Preface

We are pleased to bring you the third edition of *Culinary Math*. You are about to embark on a wonderful journey that links the world of mathematics to the culinary profession. Cooking is considered an art, yet if you are creating your art with the intention of making a living, you need to apply some of the math fundamentals discussed in this text to be successful. The purpose of this book is to guide you in understanding and appropriately using the math of the food-service industry.

This edition has been improved and enriched to meet the needs of future food-service professionals. In this edition we have updated and improved the practice problems, clarified content, and added new photography. Our most exciting addition to the third edition of *Culinary Math* is your opportunity to go to a Web site (http://www.wiley.com/go/culinarymath) where you can practice food costing (Chapter 11, page 154) on an Excel food cost form. We felt it was necessary to recognize the increasing use of computers in the food-service industry, particularly with food costing, and offer you a chance to become familiar with it while studying culinary math.

Organization of the Book

This textbook is designed to help you master the topics of culinary math. Once you have worked through the chapters in this text, you should feel confident costing out recipes, converting recipe sizes, and working with kitchen ratios. Each individual chapter is designed to move toward these goals one step at a time. These chapters build on one another, so it is important to be comfortable with the material covered in earlier chapters to be successful with the later material. Chapter 1 (page 1) reviews the basic math necessary to be able to successfully master the math in the remaining chapters. Chapter 2 (page 25) covers the units of measure used in most of the professional kitchens in the United States, and Chapter 3 (page 40) is dedicated to the metric system. It is very important to commit these units of measure and their conversions to memory to be able to work efficiently in the kitchen.

Chapters 4 and 5 (pages 49 and 60 respectively) cover converting units of measure within weight and volume, and Chapter 6 (page 71) discusses converting between weight and volume measures. Chapter 7 (page 87) presents the concept of yield percent and how it is calculated. Chapter 8 (page 106) addresses how to use yield percent to determine how much of a product is usable and how to order the correct amount of a product for a particular need. Chapters 9 and 10 (pages 120 and 138, respectively) examine how to calculate the cost and the edible portion cost, and Chapter 11 (page 154) combines these concepts in recipe costing. Chapter 12 (page 176) addresses when yield percent is ignored in ordering and costing. These situations are exceptions to the rules covered in Chapter 7 through 11. How to identify these unique circumstances and formulate the math to find the solutions is covered. Chapter 13 (page 186) deals with beverage calculations and costing. Chapter 14 (page 200) deals with changing the yield of a recipe. Chapters 15 (page 222) introduces kitchen ratios, which are ratios that are specific to the food-service industry.

Organization of Each Chapter

Each chapter begins with a short vignette describing a situation that might be encountered in the food-service industry, which connects the math in the chapter with a real-world application. The chapter objectives make you aware of the material to be covered in the chapter so that you can be sure you have met these objectives. Each chapter includes a lesson and one or more example problems designed to show a method for solving a given problem. The procedures that are demonstrated reflect tried-and-true methods that have been presented successfully for more than fifteen years; however, there are usually several ways to solve a problem, and if you perform different calculations but your solution matches the answer in the book, then you are probably on the right track. At the end of each chapter there are practice problems for you to do on your own.

How Best to Use the Practice Problems

All of the work that you do for the practice problems should be shown so that errors may be easily identified and corrected. When all the work is done on your calculator, there is no way to backtrack and find errors, which can be a very effective learning tool. Knowing how and why to make the calculations is as important as coming up with the right answer. The correct answers for the odd-numbered problems are provided for you in the back of the book so that you can check your calculations and gauge your understanding of the concepts presented in the chapter. For additional practice in recipe costing beyond the practice problems, you can access an interactive Excel food cost form online at http://www.wiley.com/go/culinarymath.

The applied math of the culinary field is both challenging and rewarding. Do not forget to use common sense when reading through the chapters, studying the examples, and doing the practice problems.

Math Basics

The understanding of numbers and how to correctly complete basic math operations with all forms of numbers is the foundation of culinary math. Food costing, recipe size conversion, recipe development, and cost control begin with the basic math concepts covered in this chapter. Errors in basic math calculations can become costly and time-consuming. It is necessary for your success to master these skills before tackling the math of the kitchen.

The primary goal of this chapter is to review basic math, including whole numbers, fractions, and decimals. After completing the basic review, the chapter covers percents and then word problems and their solutions. This chapter is designed to be a resource that may be used as a reference for the subsequent chapters.

OBJECTIVES

- Identify the place value of a whole number.

- Convert a whole number to a fraction.

- Identify the types of fractions.

- Convert a mixed number to an improper fraction.

- Convert fractions to decimals and decimals to fractions.

- Solve an equation with fractions and decimals.

- Convert a percent to a decimal or fraction and a decimal or fraction to a percent.

- Solve word problems for the part, whole, or percent.

- Round given numbers based on the situation.

WHOLE NUMBERS

Whole numbers are the counting numbers and 0. They are 0, 1, 2, 3, 4, 5, and so on. The following chart identifies the place value of whole numbers.

WHOLE NUMBERS														
Trillions			**Billions**			**Millions**			**Thousands**			**Units**		
hundreds	tens	ones	hundreds	tens	ones	hundreds	tens	ones	hundreds	tens	ones	hundreds	tens	ones

It is important to be familiar with place value when dealing with whole number operations.

FRACTIONS

Fractions are numeric symbols of the relationship between the part and the whole. They are composed of a numerator (the top number in a fraction) and a denominator (the bottom number in a fraction). Fractions are frequently used in the kitchen. Measuring cups, measuring spoons, and the volumes and weights of products ordered may be expressed in fractional quantities. Most ingredients in the recipes or formulas found in a kitchen or in a cookbook express quantities in fractional form. The fractions used in the kitchen are, for the most part, the more common fractions: $\frac{1}{8}$, $\frac{1}{4}$, $\frac{1}{3}$, $\frac{1}{2}$, $\frac{2}{3}$, $\frac{3}{4}$. A culinary recipe or formula would most likely never use a fraction such as $\frac{349}{940}$ cup of flour. However, when making calculations to increase or decrease a recipe's yield, you will be confronted with fractions that have to be converted to a measure that is more realistic in the kitchen.

A fraction may be thought of as:

- A part of a whole number: 3 out of 5 slices of pie could be presented as $\frac{3}{5}$. In this example, 3 is the part and 5 is the whole.

- An expression of a relationship between two numbers:

  $\dfrac{3}{7}$ The *numerator,* or top number
  The *denominator,* or bottom number

- A division problem: The fraction $\frac{3}{7}$ can also be written as the division problem 3 ÷ 7.

2

TYPES OF FRACTIONS

A *proper (common) fraction* is a fraction in which the numerator is less than the denominator. For example:

$$\frac{1}{2} \quad \text{and} \quad \frac{3}{4}$$

An *improper fraction* is a fraction with a numerator that is greater than or equal to the denominator, such as:

$$\frac{28}{7}, \frac{140}{70}, \quad \text{and} \quad \frac{28}{28}$$

A *mixed number* is a number that contains both a whole number and a fraction, such as:

$$4\frac{3}{8}$$

A *lowest-term fraction* is the result of reducing a fraction so that the numerator and the denominator have no other common factors beside 1. For example:

$$\frac{14}{28} = \frac{14 \div 14}{28 \div 14} = \frac{1}{2}$$

The fraction $^{14}/_{28}$ is a proper fraction, but it is not in lowest terms. Both 14 and 28 share the following factors: 2, 7, and 14. If you divide both 14 and 28 by the largest factor, 14, the result is $^{1}/_{2}$, which is equivalent to $^{14}/_{28}$.

The result of reducing a fraction so that the numerator and the denominator no longer have any common factors is a fraction expressed in its lowest terms, or lowest-term fraction.

CONVERTING FRACTIONS

CONVERTING WHOLE NUMBERS TO FRACTIONS: To convert a whole number to a fraction, place the whole number over 1.

EXAMPLE: $5 \rightarrow \dfrac{5}{1}$

CONVERTING IMPROPER FRACTIONS TO MIXED NUMBERS: To convert an improper fraction to a mixed number, divide the numerator by the denominator. The quotient will be the whole number, and the remainder (if any) will be placed over the denominator of the original improper fraction to form the fractional part of the mixed number.

> **WARNING**
> Remember that when dividing, the numerator is the number being divided.
>
> Numerator ÷ Denominator
> or
> Denominator $\overline{)\text{Numerator}}$

$$\frac{23}{5} = 5\overline{)23} \begin{array}{c} 4 \\ \end{array} = 4\frac{3}{5}$$
$$\underline{-20}$$
$$3$$

$$\frac{239}{43} = 43\overline{)239} \begin{array}{c} 5 \\ \end{array} = 5\frac{24}{43}$$
$$\underline{-215}$$
$$24$$

STEPS TO CONVERTING MIXED NUMBERS TO IMPROPER FRACTIONS

STEP 1. Multiply the whole number by the denominator.

STEP 2. Add the result to the numerator.

STEP 3. Place the resulting number over the original denominator.

Convert $4\frac{2}{3}$ to an improper fraction.

STEP 1. Multiply 4 and 3. $4\frac{2}{3}$ $4 \times 3 = 12$

STEP 2. Add 2 to the result. $4\frac{2}{3}$ $12 + 2 = 14$

STEP 3. Use 14 from step 2 as the numerator and 3 as the denominator.

$$\frac{14}{3} = 4\frac{2}{3}$$

Note that the denominator is the same in both the improper fraction and the mixed number.

ADDITION OF FRACTIONS

Fractions that are added to one another must have the same denominator (common denominator).

$\dfrac{1}{7} + \dfrac{2}{7} = \dfrac{3}{7}$

7 is the common denominator.

$$\text{Solve } \frac{5}{7} + \frac{1}{4}$$

To solve this example, first find a common denominator. There are two ways to do this:

1. MULTIPLY THE TWO DENOMINATORS TOGETHER: To find the common denominator for $\frac{5}{7}$ and $\frac{1}{4}$, multiply the first denominator, 7, by the second denominator, 4: $(7 \times 4) = 28$. The numerator of each fraction must be multiplied by the same number as the denominator was multiplied by, so that the value of the fraction remains the same. In this example, multiply the 5 by 4 and multiply the 1 by 7. Thus:

$$\frac{5}{7} = \frac{5 \times 4}{7 \times 4} = \frac{20}{28}$$

$$\frac{1}{4} = \frac{1 \times 7}{4 \times 7} = \frac{7}{28}$$

$$\frac{20}{28} + \frac{7}{28} = \frac{27}{28}$$

2. DETERMINE IF ONE DENOMINATOR IS THE FACTOR OF THE OTHER: Especially in recipes, it is not unusual for the denominator of one fraction to be evenly divisible by the denominator in the other fraction. In the following example, 16 can be divided by 8, so 8 can be used as the common denominator. This method can save time but will work only when one of the denominators is a factor of the other:

$$\frac{1}{8} + \frac{5}{16} = \frac{1 \times 2}{8 \times 2} + \frac{5}{16} = \frac{2}{16} + \frac{5}{16} = \frac{7}{16}$$

SUBTRACTION OF FRACTIONS

Fractions that are subtracted from one another must also have a common denominator. The same methods used for converting denominators to common denominators when adding fractions can be used when subtracting fractions.

EXAMPLES:
$$\frac{3}{8} - \frac{1}{8} = \frac{2}{8} = \frac{1}{4}$$

$$\frac{7}{8} - \frac{5}{9} = \frac{7 \times 9}{8 \times 9} - \frac{5 \times 8}{9 \times 8} = \frac{63}{72} - \frac{40}{72} = \frac{23}{72}$$

MULTIPLICATION OF FRACTIONS

The process of multiplying fractions simply requires that the numerators be multiplied together and the denominators be multiplied together; the results of the multiplied numerators are placed over the results of the multiplied denominators.

5

Any mixed numbers must first be converted to improper fractions before multiplying them.

$$\frac{\text{Numerator} \times \text{Numerator}}{\text{Denominator} \times \text{Denominator}} = \frac{NN}{DD}$$

EXAMPLES: $\dfrac{4}{7} \times \dfrac{3}{5} = \dfrac{12}{35}$

$1\dfrac{1}{2} \times \dfrac{1}{5} \times \dfrac{1}{7} = \dfrac{3}{2} \times \dfrac{1}{5} \times \dfrac{1}{7} = \dfrac{3}{70}$

DIVISION OF FRACTIONS

To divide fractions, first convert any mixed numbers to improper fractions. Next, invert the second fraction (the divisor) by placing the denominator on top of the numerator. Finally, change the division sign to a multiplication sign and complete the equation as a multiplication problem.

REMEMBER
A common denominator is not required when multiplying or dividing fractions.

EXAMPLES: $\dfrac{3}{4} \div 1\dfrac{2}{3} = \dfrac{3}{4} \div \dfrac{5}{3} = \dfrac{3}{4} \times \dfrac{3}{5} = \dfrac{9}{20}$

$\dfrac{7}{1} \div \dfrac{3}{4} = \dfrac{7}{1} \times \dfrac{4}{3} = \dfrac{28}{3} = 9\dfrac{1}{3}$

DECIMALS

Decimals are another common style of number that is often found in the food-service industry. For example:

- Metric quantities are expressed in decimal form.

- Money is expressed in decimal form.

- Digital scales express weight in decimal form.

- Most calculators use decimal forms of numbers.

A *decimal number* is a number that uses a decimal point and place value to show values less than 1. Like the fraction, a decimal is the representation of a part of the whole. Decimals are expressed in powers of 10. A period (.), called a *decimal point,* is used to indicate the decimal form of the number.

PLACE VALUES

The first four place values to the right of the decimal point are as follows:

DECIMAL PLACES				
	tenths	hundredths	thousandths	ten-thousandths
0 .	_	_	_	_

EXAMPLES:

$$\frac{1}{10} = 0.1$$

$$\frac{9}{100} = 0.09$$

$$\frac{89}{1000} = 0.089$$

$$\frac{321}{10,000} = 0.0321$$

A *repeating* or *recurring decimal* is the result of converting a fraction to a decimal that repeats. If you convert $^1/_3$ to a decimal, the result is $0.333333\ldots$ (a repeating decimal in which the 3 goes on infinitely). To record a repeating decimal, you can put a bar over the first set of repeating digits.

ADDITION AND SUBTRACTION OF DECIMALS

The decimal points and place values must be aligned when adding and subtracting decimal values. For instance, if you are adding 0.14 and 0.5, it is important to remember that you can only add numbers of the same place value. So, you must add the 1 to the 5, since they are both in the tenths place. The answer to this problem is 0.64, not 0.19.

EXAMPLES: $3.14 + 18.4 + 340.1 + 200.147 =$

$$\begin{array}{r} 3.14 \\ 18.4 \\ 340.1 \\ +\,200.147 \\ \hline 561.787 \end{array}$$

and $9.736 - 6.5 =$

$$\begin{array}{r} 9.736 \\ -\,6.5 \\ \hline 3.236 \end{array}$$

7

MULTIPLICATION OF DECIMALS

When you are multiplying decimals, first, multiply as though they were whole numbers. Then mark off from right to left the same number of decimal places as found in both the multiplier and the multiplicand (number multiplied) and place the point in your answer (the product).

Multiplicand
× Multiplier
Product

If, for example, you are multiplying 40.8 by 3.02, you would first do the multiplication as if there were no decimal points (408 × 302) and then count how many *decimal places*, or numbers to the right of the decimal point, there are. In this case, one number (8) is to the right of the decimal point in 40.8, and two numbers (02) are to the right in 3.02. This makes a total of three decimal places, so in the product we would insert the decimal point so that there are three numbers to the right of the decimal point.

EXAMPLE:
$$40.8 \times 3.02 = 40.8 = 1 \text{ decimal place}$$
$$\times 3.02 = 2 \text{ decimal places}$$
$$816$$
$$+ \underline{122400}$$
$$123.216 = 3 \text{ decimal places}$$

DIVISION OF DECIMALS

As with multiplication, you are first going to divide decimals as you divide whole numbers:

$$\text{Divisor} \overline{)\text{Dividend}}^{\text{Quotient}}$$

There are five steps in dividing decimals:

STEP 1. Set up the division problem as you would if you were dividing whole numbers.

STEP 2. Move the decimal point of the divisor to the right (if it is not already a whole number) so that you have a whole number. This will eliminate a decimal in the divisor.

STEP 3. Move the decimal point in the dividend the same number of places to the right. If you need to move the decimal more places than there are digits, add zeros to accommodate this move.

8

STEP 4. Place another decimal point right above the decimal's new position in the dividend. This places the decimal point in your answer (quotient).

STEP 5. Divide as though you are dividing whole numbers, disregarding the decimal points. Be careful to keep the digits in the same place values lined up as you divide. For the purposes of this text, dividing to the ten-thousandths place is sufficient.

$$8.325 \div 2.25 = 225\overline{)832.5}$$

$$
\begin{array}{r}
3.7 \\
225\overline{)832.5} \\
-675 \\
\hline
1575 \\
-1575 \\
\hline
0
\end{array}
$$

$$12 \div 1.5 = 15\overline{)120}$$

$$
\begin{array}{r}
8 \\
15\overline{)120}
\end{array}
$$

CONVERTING FRACTIONS TO DECIMALS

To convert a fraction to its equivalent decimal number, carry out the division to the ten-thousandths place and truncate. *Truncate* means to cut off a number at a given decimal place without regard to rounding (for example, 12.34567 truncated to the hundredths place would be 12.34).

Convert ½ to decimal form. $2\overline{)1.0}$

$$
\begin{array}{r}
0.5 \\
2\overline{)1.0}
\end{array}
$$

CONVERTING DECIMALS TO FRACTIONS

To convert a decimal number to a fraction:

STEP 1. Read the number as a decimal using place value.

STEP 2. Write the number as a fraction.

STEP 3. Reduce to lowest terms.

9

Convert 0.0075 to a fraction.

STEP 1. Seventy-five ten-thousandths

STEP 2. $\dfrac{75}{10,000}$

STEP 3. $\dfrac{75}{10,000} = \dfrac{3}{400}$

PERCENT

A *percent* is a ratio of a number to 100; the symbol for percent is %. A *ratio* is a comparison of two numbers or the quotient of two numbers. A ratio can be expressed as a fraction, a division problem, or an expression, such as $\frac{3}{5}$, 3 ÷ 5, or 3 to 5. The term *percent* means "part of one hundred"; thus, 7 percent means 7 parts out of every 100. Like fractions and decimals, percent is an expression of the relationship between part and whole. If 34 percent of the customers in a restaurant favor nutritious entrées, a part (34) of a whole number of customers (100) is being expressed. With percents, the whole is *always* 100. In this example, all of the customers that enter the restaurant represent 100 percent.

The use of percent to express a rate is common practice in the food-service industry. For example, food and beverage costs, labor costs, operating costs, fixed costs, and profits are usually stated as a percent to establish standards of control. Additionally, in a kitchen or bakeshop percent is used to find yield percent and bakers' percent, which will be covered in later chapters.

To indicate that a number is a percent, the number must be accompanied by the word *percent* or a percent sign (%).

CONVERTING DECIMALS TO PERCENTS

To convert a decimal to a percent, multiply the number by 100 and add a percent sign.

EXAMPLE: $0.25 = 0.25 \times 100 = 25\%$

A shortcut would be simply to move the decimal point two places to the right and add a percent sign.

CONVERTING PERCENTS TO DECIMALS

To convert percents to decimal form, divide by 100 and drop the percent sign.

EXAMPLE: $30\% = \dfrac{30}{100} = 0.30$

10

A shortcut would be simply to move the decimal point two places to the left and drop the percent sign.

If there is a fraction in the percent, first change that fraction to a decimal.

EXAMPLE: $37\dfrac{1}{4}\%$

$37\dfrac{1}{4}\% = 37.25\%$

37.25% converts to 0.3725

PERCENT TO DECIMAL AND PERCENT TO FRACTION FLOWCHART

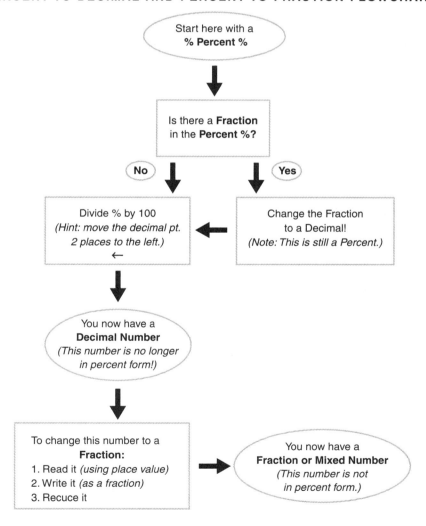

PERCENTS IN THE KITCHEN

In the kitchen it is often necessary for the chef to work with percents. Chefs may use percents to calculate and apply a yield percent or food cost percent. In these cases it is helpful to remember the following formulas.

$$\textbf{PERCENT} = \frac{\text{Part}}{\text{Whole}}$$

$$\textbf{PART} = \text{Whole} \times \text{Percent}$$

$$\textbf{WHOLE} = \frac{\text{Part}}{\text{Percent}}$$

Hints for using formulas involving percents:

- The number or word that follows the word *of* is usually the whole number and the word *is* usually is connected to the part. What is 20 percent of 70? In this example, *of* 70 implies that 70 is the whole; 20 is the percent. The *what is* implies that the part is the unknown and what you are solving for.

- The percent will always be identified with either the symbol % or the word *percent*.

- The part will usually be less than the whole.

- Before trying to solve the problem, identify the part, whole, and percent and which you need to solve for.

THE PERCENT TRIANGLE

The following triangle is a tool used to find part, whole, or percent. Rather than memorizing the three separate formulas provided in the preceding section, many students find the following triangle helpful and easy to remember.

STEPS FOR USING THE PERCENT TRIANGLE

STEP 1. Determine what you are looking for—part, whole, or percent.

STEP 2. *To find the part*
Cover the *P* for part.
W and % are side by side. This directs you to multiply the whole by the percent. (Remember first to change the percent to a decimal by dividing by 100.)

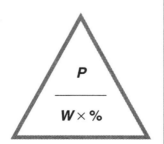

To find the whole
Cover the *W* for whole.
P is over %. This directs you to divide the part by the percent. (Remember first to change the percent to a decimal by dividing by 100.)

To find the percent
Cover the % for percent.
P is over *W*. This directs you to divide the part by the whole and multiply the answer by 100 to convert it to the percent.

ROUNDING

Rounding is an important basic math skill. In the world of mathematics, rounding is predominantly a numeric concept (5 or more rounds up and 4 or less rounds down). Many basic math textbooks contain exercises that have the students practice rounding to a specific place value. In the applied math needed in the food-service industry, however, it is far more important to consider the situation before rounding. When dealing with money, for example, it is important to round to the cent or the hundredths place. Determining to round up or down is clearly dependent on the situation. Whether you choose to round up or down can affect the outcome dramatically. In the food-service industry, the number you rounded may be multiplied by a very large number. If you have rounded incorrectly, the answer could result in a large loss of income, several people going hungry at a party you are catering, or not having enough of a particular ingredient. Rounding will be covered more specifically in the chapters to follow.

SOLVING WORD PROBLEMS

Word problems are good practice for applied math because they use real-life situations. Below is a list of steps designed to break down the process of solving word problems into manageable pieces.

STEPS TO SOLVING WORD PROBLEMS

STEP 1. Determine what is being solved for.

STEP 2. Decide what must be done to get the answer.

STEP 3. Perform the necessary calculations.

STEP 4. Find out if the question has been answered by the calculations.

STEP 5. Decide whether the answer is reasonable.

In culinary math, step 5 takes on a whole new meaning because it is related to real situations dealing with food. For instance, a problem could ask how many apple pies should be made for dinner if 40 percent of your customers usually order a slice of apple pie. Each pie is cut into 8 slices, and you are expecting 240 customers this evening. After you complete the calculations, your answer indicates that you need 240 pies. At this point you should ask yourself if this answer makes sense given the other information you have. If you are expecting 240 customers, this would mean that the number you arrived at allows for one pie per person; clearly something is wrong with the calculations. When this occurs, you should go over your work to find where the error was made. Your ability to find errors will indicate a clear understanding of the concept and facilitate your learning. If you pay close attention to making sure your answer makes sense, it is clear to see that the correct answer is 12 pies.

CHAPTER REVIEW

Basic math is the foundation for all of the math covered in this text. Understanding the concepts covered is the key to your success in culinary math. As you complete the work in this chapter, make sure that you have a good handle on these concepts. You should refer back to this chapter as you progress through the book, if needed.

CHAPTER PRACTICE

Answers to odd-numbered questions may be found on page 251.

Calculate the following. Reduce your answer to lowest terms.

1. $\dfrac{1}{2} + \dfrac{1}{8} =$

2. $\dfrac{1}{6} + \dfrac{1}{5} =$

3. $6\dfrac{1}{6} + \dfrac{1}{4} =$

4. $\dfrac{2}{3} + \dfrac{3}{4} =$

5. $10 + \dfrac{1}{9} + \dfrac{2}{3} =$

6. $\dfrac{2}{10} - \dfrac{1}{6} =$

7. $\dfrac{1}{2} - \dfrac{1}{8} =$

8. $7\dfrac{3}{8} - \dfrac{2}{24} =$

9. $\dfrac{5}{6} \times \dfrac{2}{3} =$

10. $15 \times \dfrac{4}{5} =$

11. $1\frac{3}{4} \times 4\frac{3}{8} =$

12. $\frac{1}{2} \div \frac{1}{4} =$

13. $\frac{1}{4} \div \frac{7}{8} =$

14. $1\frac{1}{2} \div 6 =$

15. $1\frac{3}{8} \div 6\frac{7}{10} =$

Is the answer reasonable? Complete the following chart.

Question	Answer	Unreasonable Because	Answer Should Be Approximately
16. What is your salary per month for your full-time job?	$32.41		
17. You have 3 pints of strawberries. Each cake requires 1½ pints. How many cakes can you make?	6 cakes		
18. You have 20 pounds of dough. Each loaf requires ¾ pound of dough. How many loaves can you make?	2 loaves		
19. How much do you pay in rent each month?	$32.41		
20. How many customers did you serve last night?	3.02		
21. What is the check average in your restaurant?	$0.29		
22. How many total hours did the dishwasher work this week?	168 hours		

15

Convert the following fractions into their decimal equivalent.

EXAMPLE: $\dfrac{1}{2} = 0.5$

23. $\dfrac{3}{2} =$ **24.** $\dfrac{3}{8} =$ **25.** $\dfrac{9}{18} =$

26. $\dfrac{5}{16} =$ **27.** $\dfrac{2}{5} =$ **28.** $\dfrac{7}{8} =$

29. $\dfrac{6}{24} =$ **30.** $\dfrac{3}{48} =$ **31.** $\dfrac{26}{5} =$

32. $\dfrac{66}{10} =$ **33.** $\dfrac{440}{100} =$ **34.** $\dfrac{4400}{1000} =$

Solve the following. If your answer has more than four decimal places, drop all digits past four places (truncate). Do not round the answer.

35. $3.6024 + 18.32 + 51.05 + 2.5 =$

_____

_____

_____

_____

_____

36. $0.0365 + 0.001 + 0.999 =$

_____

_____

_____

_____

_____

37. $9.765 - 4.0631 =$

_____

_____

_____

_____

_____

38. $1.2634 - 0.99 =$

39. $78 \div 0.0347 =$

40. $0.025 \div 98.75 =$

41. $91.30 \div 40 =$

42. $0.32 \times 1.1 =$

43. $0.065 \times 2.001 =$

_____

_____

_____

_____

_____

44. $42 \times 1.5 =$

_____

_____

_____

_____

_____

Find the decimal equivalent for the following:

45. 7285% **46.** 9.99% **47.** $\frac{1}{4}\%$

48. 100% **49.** 0.5% **50.** 25%

Change these numbers to percents.

51. 0.0125 **52.** 9.99 **53.** 0.00001

54. $\frac{2}{5}$ **55.** $1\frac{1}{8}$

Complete the following table. If your answer has more than four decimal places, drop all digits past four places (truncate). Do not round or reduce the answer.

	Decimal	Fraction	Percent
56.		$\dfrac{5}{6}$	
57.	0.009		
58.			$7\dfrac{3}{4}\%$
59.	1.23		
60.			0.45%
61.		$\dfrac{7}{8}$	

For the following table, the given situations present a number that is a result of mathematical calculations. However, these numbers do not necessarily make sense in a kitchen. Determine if the situation requires the number to be rounded up or down, and give an explanation.

The Situation	Round Up? Write Correct Answer	Round Down? Write Correct Answer	Explanation
62. A case of zucchini will serve 76.8 people. How many people can you serve?			
63. A magnum of wine will fill 12.675 glasses with 4 ounces of wine. How many glasses will you be able to sell from this bottle?			
64. You need 6.4 pounds of onions for a recipe. How many pounds should you purchase?			
65. You have calculated a selling price of $12.2704 for the special of the day. How much should you charge for this special?			

19

The Situation	Round Up? Write Correct Answer	Round Down? Write Correct Answer	Explanation
66. 68.65% of a mango is usable. What percent can you use?			
67. 13.374 pies will be necessary to serve the guests at a party you are catering. How many pies should you bake?			
68. 1½ teaspoons of cumin costs $0.0439. How much does the cumin cost?			
69. 5¼ watermelons are needed to make fruit salad. How many watermelons should you order?			

Solve each of the following word problems. Show your work. For percent answers, round to the nearest tenth percent. Any partial pennies, round up.

70. A restaurant purchases 40 pounds of potatoes. Twenty percent of the potatoes are peels. How many pounds of potatoes are peels?

_____
_____
_____
_____
_____

71. If you order 300 lobster tails and you use 32 percent, how many do you have left?

_____
_____
_____
_____
_____

72. You made 400 rolls, which is 40 percent of what you have to make. What is the total number of rolls you have to make?

_____

_____

_____

_____

_____

73. You have 60 percent of a bottle of raspberry syrup remaining. If 10 fluid ounces were used, how many fluid ounces did the bottle originally hold?

_____

_____

_____

_____

_____

74. Out of 250 cakes, you use 34 percent for a party. How many cakes are left over?

_____

_____

_____

_____

_____

75. What percent discount would you have gotten if the actual price of an item was $16.95 and you paid $15.96?

_____

_____

_____

_____

_____

76. Annual recycling costs are $7,000. Annual sales amount to $1,185,857. What percent of sales does recycling cost represent?

_____

_____

_____

_____

_____

77. You have a bakeshop staff of 30, which is 20 percent of your total staff. How many members do you have on your total staff?

_____

_____

_____

_____

_____

78. If a caterer receives an order for 2,800 canapés at $0.06 each and he requires 30 percent down, how much will the client owe after the deposit is paid?

_____

_____

_____

_____

_____

79. You paid $508 for a new piece of equipment _after_ a 9 percent discount. What was the original price? Round your answer to the nearest cent.

_____

_____

_____

_____

_____

80. Bob makes a pot of coffee. By 10:00 A.M. only 3 cups remain. If 85 percent of the coffee has been consumed, how many cups of coffee did the pot originally hold?

_____

_____

_____

_____

_____

81. You are serving 3 different entrées at a party you are catering. If 100 guests are having beef, 175 guests are having pasta, and 45 percent of the guests are having chicken, how many guests are expected at this party?

_____

_____

_____

_____

_____

82. A case of apples you received has 12 rotten apples in it. If this represents 25 percent of the entire case, how many apples were in the case?

_____

_____

_____

_____

_____

83. Mr. Smith purchased $125.00 worth of spices and herbs. Because this was such a large order, the supplier charged Mr. Smith only $95.00. What percent discount did Mr. Smith receive?

_____

_____

_____

_____

_____

84. Betty usually charges $0.85 per piece for mini appetizers. For a large party she charges her customers $680 for a thousand mini appetizers. What percent discount was Betty offering?

_____

_____

_____

_____

_____

85. You are catering a dinner party for 25 guests. Each guest will be served a ramekin of chocolate mousse. If only 18 guests show up, what percent of the mousse will be left over?

_____

_____

_____

_____

_____

86. There are 47 people working in your café. Twenty-nine employees are part time. What percent of your employees are full time? Round your answer to the nearest tenth of a percent.

_____

_____

_____

_____

_____

Customary Units of Measure 2

When you work in a kitchen, it is necessary to know the units of measure and the relationship between the units. Many of the measuring devices found in a kitchen may not have markings on them, and you will need to know the relative size of measuring containers to be able to distinguish one from another. For instance, if a recipe calls for 1 quart of chicken stock, you need to be able to select the correct measuring container.

Imagine that you are working in a U.S. kitchen that is "in the weeds" (running behind in production) for lunch. You are preparing cream of broccoli soup and need 3 quarts of chicken stock. The only measuring container available is a 1-gallon container. You are aware that there are 4 quarts in 1 gallon and, therefore, $^{3}/_{4}$ of the container will equal 3 quarts. If you did not know this, you would have to take the additional time to look for a quart container and fill the quart measure three times. Knowing the units of measure will allow you to solve these problems. As a professional in the food-service industry, you will need to be very familiar with many different units of measure.

Accurate measuring in the kitchen results in better control of food costs and accuracy in production. Proper measurement improves food quality, labor utilization, and use of trim. For example, imagine that a recipe calls for $^{1}/_{8}$ ounce of saffron (a very expensive spice). However, instead of weighing the product, the cook just uses a small handful. If the cook has used too much saffron, the cost is greater than it would have been if the proper amount had been measured. Additionally, the taste of the final product will be altered by the carelessness.

OBJECTIVES

- List the names and abbreviations of the units of measure most commonly used in the food-service industry.

- Demonstrate your understanding of the relative sizes of the measuring tools used in the food-service industry.

- Recall the equivalents of volume measures without references.

- Recall the equivalents of weight measures without references.

- Explain the difference between weight and volume measurements.

- Define a fluid ounce and explain how it differs from an ounce.

MEASURING EQUIPMENT

As shown on the next page, the following pieces of measuring equipment are used most often in a professional kitchen in the United States.

Nested measuring cups are used for dry ingredients. The common sizes are 1 cup, $\frac{1}{2}$ cup, $\frac{1}{3}$ cup, and $\frac{1}{4}$ cup. Measuring cups are widely used to define the quantity of ingredients in recipes; however, measurement by weight is more accurate. For instance, if two cooks were measuring $\frac{1}{2}$ cup of brown sugar, the amount they put in their recipe might be different depending on how tightly the brown sugar is packed in the cup. If the brown sugar was weighed, there would be no discrepancy.

Graduated measuring cups may be made of plastic or aluminum and are usually used for measuring liquids. The common sizes are 1 cup, 1 pint, 1 quart, and 1 gallon.

Measuring spoons are used for dry and liquid ingredients. The common sizes are 1 tablespoon, 1 teaspoon, $\frac{1}{2}$ teaspoon, and $\frac{1}{4}$ teaspoon.

Measuring cups, from left to right: metal graduated measure, nested measuring cups, plastic graduated measure.

PROPER MEASURING TECHNIQUES

Measurement in the professional kitchen or bakeshop is critical to preparing a recipe accurately. In order to keep costs in line and ensure consistency of quality and quantity, ingredients and portion sizes must be measured correctly each time a recipe is made. There are procedures for using specific measuring devices that ensure ingredients are measured properly and with consistency.

PROCEDURE FOR USING VOLUME MEASURES

Volume is the space filled by a liquid, gas, or solid. Volume measuring devices must be filled correctly to give an accurate measure. For liquids, use graduated liquid measuring cups or pitchers and fill to the desired level. The measuring utensil must be sitting on a level, stable surface for an accurate measurement. The mark on the measuring device should be at eye level.

For dry volume measure, it is important that all ingredients be in the form called for in the recipe before measuring (i.e., ground, diced, chopped). Use nested measuring tools for dry ingredients measured by volume. Overfill the measure, and then scrape away the excess as you level off the measure. Never pack down or tamp the ingredients unless the recipe specifically instructs you to do so.

Scoops, also known as *dishers*, are used primarily for measuring portion sizes of solid products such as cookie dough, ice cream, stuffing, cooked rice, and the like. When using scoops to measure, be careful to fill them completely and level them off so that each portion is correct.

USING WEIGHT MEASURE

Weight is a measurement of the heaviness of a substance. In professional kitchens, weight is usually the preferred type of measurement because it is easier to attain accuracy with weight than it is with volume. The tool used for measuring weight is a scale. There are different types of scales: digital scales, spring scales, and balance-beam scales. To ensure correct measuring, all scales must be on a level surface and kept clean and free of debris.

If you use a container or parchment to hold ingredients as they are weighed out, place the empty container or parchment on the scale and reset it to zero (known as *to tare*). Digital scales have a tare button that resets the scale to zero. A spring scale will have a knob or dial to turn that will rotate the numbers or move the marker; in either case the marker and zero are in alignment when the scale has been properly tared. When using a balance-beam scale, place the container that is to hold the ingredient on the left-hand side of the sale. To zero out (tare) the scale, place an identical container, or an item that is the same weight as the container, on the right-hand side of the scale, and move the weight on the front of the scale to the right until the scale is balanced. To weigh ingredients on spring scales or digital scales, fill the container slowly until the desired weight shows on the readout or dial. To weigh ingredients on a balance-beam scale, adjust the weight on the front of the scale by moving it to the right the amount of notches that equals the weight to be measured, or place weights that equal the amount to be weighed on the right-hand side of the scale. Add the substance to be measured to the left-hand side of the scale until the scale is balanced.

Portion instruments, from left to right: portion scoops, measuring spoons, ladles.

Scales, from left to right: spring scale, digital scale, balance-beam scale.

Ladles are used for measuring liquid. The common sizes include 2 fluid ounces, 4 fluid ounces, and 8 fluid ounces.

Portion scoops come in a wide variety of sizes and are used to regulate single portions of finished food rather than ingredients. The scoops are numbered, and each number corresponds to the number of scoops it would take to make a quart. For instance, a number 30 scoop means that there would be 30 scoops needed to make a quart. This photograph shows a number 10 scoop, which holds 3.2 fluid ounces, a number 16 scoop, which holds 2 fluid ounces, and a number 30 scoop, which holds 1.06 fluid ounces.

The most common *scales* to measure weight in a kitchen are the digital (electronic) scale, the balance-beam scale, and the spring-loaded scale.

COMMON FOOD-SERVICE MEASURES AND ABBREVIATIONS

Common Term	Abbreviation
teaspoon	t, tsp
tablespoon	T, tbsp
cup	C, c
pint	pt
quart	qt
gallon	G, gal
fluid ounce	fl oz
ounce	oz
pound	lb, #
each	ea
bunch	bu
to taste	tt

COUNT

Count, in the culinary world, is used to determine the number of a particular ingredient used in a recipe. For instance, a recipe may call for 3 strawberries, 1 pineapple, 2 medium onions, or 1 loaf of bread. Count is often a convenient measurement because the ingredient is used in the recipe in the same unit in which it is purchased.

HINT
When using or reading volume measurement abbreviations, it is easy to confuse a capital *T* (tablespoon) and a lowercase *t* (teaspoon). To avoid mistakes, pay attention to this difference.

VOLUME

Volume measurement, as it applies to the kitchen, generally refers to the common measuring tools used in the United States, such as cups, teaspoons, and quarts. These tools are used to define the space that is filled with the products being measured. Volume measures are related to each other in a very specific way. For example, 1 cup of a substance is always equal to 16 tablespoons of the same substance, just as 1 tablespoon of a substance is always equal to 3 teaspoons of the same substance (see the following figures showing several volume

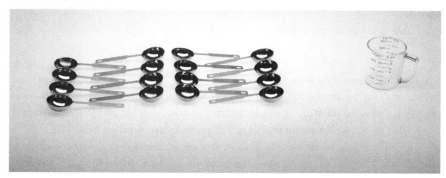

16 tablespoons is equivalent to 1 cup.

2 cups is equivalent to 1 pint.

29

2 pints is equivalent to 1 quart.

4 quarts is equivalent to 1 gallon.

measure equivalents using a liquid ingredient). Volume is a preferred method of measure for specific measuring situations. For example, small quantities of both liquid and dry ingredients are easy to measure using measuring spoons. Larger quantities of liquids are measured with volume measuring tools such as pints, quarts, and gallons. The fluid ounce is also a unit of volume measure. Many products are purchased in volume measure, such as a case of apples, a flat of raspberries, a bushel of crabs, a gallon of milk, and a pint of cream.

The following chart shows units of volume measures and their equivalents. These equivalents are always the same, regardless of what substance is being measured.

U.S. STANDARD VOLUME EQUIVALENTS

Volume Measures	Volume Equivalents
1 tablespoon	3 teaspoons
1 cup	16 tablespoons
1 pint	2 cups
1 quart	2 pints
1 gallon	4 quarts

VOLUME IN PORTIONING

When the food is ready to be served, portion scoops are often used to make the amount portioned on a plate consistent. Portion scoops are numbered. Each number relates to the number of scoops that are in 32 fluid ounces, or 1 quart. The following table gives the standard portion scoop numbers and their equivalents in fluid ounces.

SCOOP EQUIVALENTS

Scoop Number	Fluid Ounces in One Scoop
4	8
5	6.4
6	5.33
8	4
10	3.2
12	2.66
16	2
20	1.6
24	1.33
30	1.06
40	0.8
60	0.53

WEIGHT

In contrast to volume, *weight* is how heavy a substance is. Weight is determined by using a scale. In kitchens in the United States there are two units of measure most commonly used to express weight: pounds and ounces. You might occasionally come across another unit of weight, the ton, which is 2,000 pounds. As mentioned previously, weight measure is the most accurate way to ensure that the quantity is correct and consistent. Unfortunately, most recipes tend to rely on volume measures.

WEIGHT EQUIVALENT		
	1 pound = 16 ounces	

FLUID OUNCES

Some recipes list quantities of ingredients by the fluid ounce, and many ingredients are purchased and packaged by the fluid ounce. Fluid ounces refer to volume, not weight. The chart below lists the volume equivalents for fluid ounces. It is important to be familiar with these equivalents.

ADDITIONAL VOLUME EQUIVALENTS		
Volume Measure	Equivalent in Fluid Ounces	
1 tablespoon	½ fluid ounce	
1 cup	8 fluid ounces	
1 pint	16 fluid ounces	
1 quart	32 fluid ounces	
1 gallon	128 fluid ounces	

In this book, fluid ounces are labeled differently than weight ounces. This is not necessarily the case in the real world. Unfortunately, many measuring tools, packages, and recipes use these two very different measures interchangeably. Be aware of this, and use common sense to prevent culinary disasters.

THE OUNCE CONFUSION

Many people believe that 1 cup of any ingredient always weighs 8 ounces, no matter what is in the cup. In truth, only 1 cup (8 fluid ounces) of water or water-like liquids (liquids that have the same density as water) will assuredly weigh 8 ounces. If something other than water or a water-like liquid is measured in a cup, it will still equal 8 fluid ounces, but it will not necessarily weigh 8 ounces.

This confusion comes from not distinguishing the term *ounce* from the term *fluid ounce*. An ounce is something that you weigh, and a fluid ounce is a volume measure. The measurement for 1 fluid ounce is derived from the amount of space needed to hold a quantity of water weighing 1 ounce. Fluid ounces and ounces are the same only when the ingredient being measured has the same density as water.

Some examples of water-like liquids include alcohol, juices, vinegar, and oil (actually, oil is lighter than water, but the difference is so small that it is ignored in culinary applica-

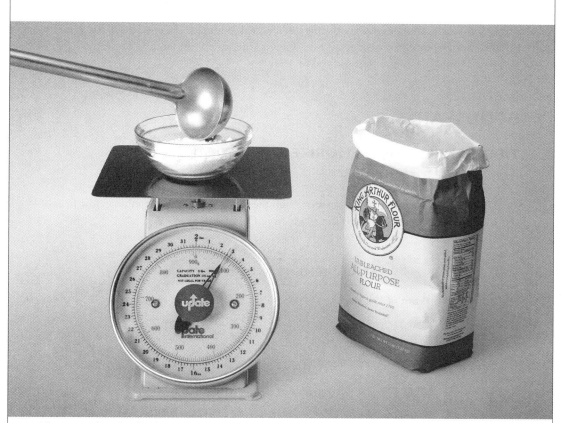

Many people mistakenly use a ladle to measure ingredients in ounces. Ladles measure in fluid ounces. If a 4-fluid-ounce ladle (equivalent to ½ cup) were used to measure flour, the quantity in the ladle would weigh only about 2½ ounces (see figure above).

tions). In instances such as these, the terms *fluid ounce* and *ounce* may be used interchangeably. On the contrary, when a recipe calls for a liquid such as honey, corn syrup, molasses, maple syrup, or heavy cream, you must pay close attention to the type of measure called for. One cup or 8 fluid ounces of any of these substances will not weigh 8 ounces (for example, 8 fluid ounces of honey weighs 12 ounces), and results will vary significantly if the terms are used interchangeably.

CHAPTER REVIEW

To work efficiently in a kitchen and prepare food products successfully, it is necessary to learn units of measure and their equivalents. The measurements discussed in this chapter are currently used in the majority of commercial kitchens in the United States. If you are planning to go anywhere else in the world to cook, you will also need to know the metric system (see Chapter 3, page 40).

Weight is generally the more accurate unit of measure. There is a difference between fluid ounces, a unit of volume, and ounces, a unit of weight. Many manufacturers, when printing the measurements on measuring devices, will omit *fl* (the abbreviation for *fluid*) before the word *ounce* on an item clearly designed to measure fluid ounces. The culinary professional should use common sense and be alert.

STUDY AIDS

TIPS TO HELP YOU MEMORIZE THE EQUIVALENTS

1. Make flash cards using index cards or small pieces of paper and the table below to assist you. There will be more study cards added in Chapter 3, page 45.

MEASUREMENT STUDY CARDS	
Front of the Card	**Back of the Card**
1 tbsp = _____ tsp	1 tbsp = ___3___ tsp
1 cup = _____ tbsp	1 cup = ___16___ tbsp
1 cup = _____ tsp	1 cup = ___48___ tsp
1 pt = _____ cups	1 pt = ___2___ cups
1 gal = _____ qt	1 gal = ___4___ qt
1 gal = _____ pt	1 gal = ___8___ pt
1 gal = _____ cups	1 gal = ___16___ cups
1 cup of water = _____ fl oz	1 cup of water = ___8___ fl oz
1 quart of water = _____ fl oz	1 quart of water = ___32___ fl oz
1 gal of water = _____ fl oz	1 gal of water = ___128___ fl oz
1 tbsp of water = _____ fl oz	1 tbsp of water = ___$\frac{1}{2}$___ fl oz
1 pound = _____ oz	1 pound = ___16___ oz

2. Practice using the flash cards until you know the measurements and their equivalents quickly and without error. One way to do this is to make two piles: the ones you know and the ones that you do not know. Practice until all the cards are in the pile of the ones you know.

3. Study in groups. Using the flash cards, flip a card down onto the table. Whoever says the equivalent first keeps the card. Quiz each other with the cards you have in your hand, because those will be the cards your studymates don't know as well as you do.

4. If you have access to an equipment storage room, become familiar with the measuring containers. Take out all of the measuring containers you can find. Fill the largest container with water and see how many times you can fill the smaller containers. You may also want to weigh a container filled with various ingredients on the scale. (Many people are visual learners and find it helpful to see the relationships between these measures.)

5. Use study aids such as those shown in the following figures.

34

Graphic study aids help for a more visual memorization and understanding. Shown here is the relationship between a gallon, quart, pint, and cup.

BUSHEL

PECK	PECK
PECK	GALLON
	GALLON

A graphic depiction of the relationship between a bushel, peck, and gallon.

CHAPTER PRACTICE

Answers to odd-numbered questions may be found on page 251.

If your answer has more than four digits after the decimal, drop all digits past four places (truncate). Do not round or reduce the answer.

1. Describe the difference between a weight measure and a volume measure.

_____

_____

_____

_____

_____

2. What is the difference between 8 fluid ounces and 1 cup?

_____

_____

_____

_____

_____

3. What is the difference between 8 ounces and 8 fluid ounces?

_____

_____

_____

_____

_____

4. What is the difference between 1 cup and 8 ounces?

_____

_____

_____

_____

_____

5. What is the difference between 1 cup and 9 ounces?

_____

_____

_____

_____

_____

6. Complete the following table:

Ingredient	Does It Weigh 8 oz in a Cup?	How Do You Know That?	Is It 8 fl oz in a Cup?	How Do You Know That?
Water				
Honey				
Flour				

7. Give an example (fact or fiction) of a situation that proves that it is imperative for you to know units of measure.

_____

_____

_____

_____

8. How many scoops can you get from a quart using a number 30 scoop?

_____

_____

_____

_____

_____

9. What is the difference between a number 8 scoop and a number 10 scoop?

_____

_____

_____

_____

_____

10. What happens to the number of fluid ounces in a scoop as the scoop number increases?

_____

_____

_____

_____

_____

11. If the scoop number relates to the number of scoops that are in 32 fluid ounces, or 1 quart, then explain how you calculate the number of fluid ounces in a number 12 scoop.

_____

_____

_____

_____

_____

Test yourself. In one minute or less, complete the following:

12. One cup is equal to _____ tablespoon(s).

13. One tablespoon is equal to _____ teaspoon(s).

14. One pint is equal to _____ cup(s).

15. One gallon is equal to _____ quart(s).

16. One quart is equal to _____ pint(s).

17. One pound is equal to _____ ounce(s).

Use your knowledge of percents (Chapter 1, page 10–13) for Questions 18–25.

18. What percent of a gallon is a pint?

_____
_____
_____
_____
_____

19. What percent of a tablespoon is a teaspoon?

_____
_____
_____
_____
_____

20. A cup is 25 percent of what measure?

_____
_____
_____
_____
_____

21. A pint is 12.5 percent of what measure?

_____
_____
_____
_____
_____

22. What percent of a cup is 3 tablespoons?

_____
_____
_____
_____
_____

23. If you have 1 cup of flour and you use 4 tablespoons, what percent is left in the cup?

_____

_____

_____

_____

_____

24. Eleven fluid ounces of water is what percent of a pint?

_____

_____

_____

_____

_____

25. If a recipe you are using calls for 2 fluid ounces of flour, how much of a cup of flour should you use in the recipe?

_____

_____

_____

_____

_____

In one minute or less, answer the following:

26. One quart is equal to _____ fluid ounce(s).

27. One tablespoon is equal to _____ fluid ounce(s).

28. One cup is equal to _____ fluid ounce(s).

29. One pint is equal to _____ fluid ounce(s).

30. One gallon is equal to _____ fluid ounce(s).

31. Your friend says to you, "I have to use 8 ounces of parsley in a recipe. I'll just measure a cup of it, right?" What would you say?

_____

_____

_____

_____

_____

Metric Measures

3

You are given a recipe to make Italian Cream Pastries while you are working for an Italian chef. The recipe calls for 100 grams of butter. You go into the walk-in and grab three cases of butter because 100 grams sure sounds like a lot. As the chef walks by, he looks at you, shakes his head, and laughs. What went wrong?

The next day the sous chef wants you to gather the mise en place for a recipe. He gives you the standard recipe that is used in the restaurant, but all the measurements are in metric amounts.

You may come across situations involving metric measures whether you are working in the United States or abroad. Many goods produced outside the United States are sold in metric amounts, and wines and spirits come bottled in metric units. This chapter explains the metric system and its relationship to the U.S. standard system as used in the food-service industry.

OBJECTIVES

- Identify the areas in food service where the metric system may be used.

- Apply the equivalents for the metric system and the U.S. standard system as they will be used in the kitchen.

- Determine the appropriate metric measure when given an ingredient in U.S. standard measure.

A liter is very similar to a quart, although not equal.

METRIC MEASURES: USES AND ADVANTAGES

The metric system is the global language of measurements that has been adopted by almost every country. The United States is one of the few countries that has not fully adopted the metric system. There are a number of kitchen situations in which knowledge of the metric system is important. The following are a few examples:

- Working in a country where the measurement of choice is metric

- Ordering ingredients from overseas that are packaged in metric amounts

- Calculating nutritional information

- Measuring wines and spirits

- Using recipes from countries where ingredients are listed in metric quantities

There are many advantages to using metric measures:

- The metric system is an internationally recognized system of measure.

- The system is based on the number 10, which makes calculating easier.

- Recording very small measures is easier and therefore more accurate.

THE METRIC SYSTEM

The following table gives the standard abbreviations for the metric measurements that are used in the food-service industry.

41

Metric Base Unit Abbreviations	Other Common Metric Abbreviations
liter, L	milliliter, mL
gram, g	kilogram, kg

The metric system is a system based on the number 10. The following table lists the common metric prefixes and their relationship to the base unit—grams, liters, or meters.

METRIC PREFIXES

kilo- = 1,000 base units
deka- = 10 base units
deci- = 0.1 base unit
centi- = 0.01 base unit
milli- = 0.001 base unit

Base Unit	Kilo-	Deka-	Deci-	Centi-	Milli-
gram	kilogram	dekagram	decigram	centigram	milligram
liter	kiloliter	dekaliter	deciliter	centiliter	milliliter

The commonly used metric unit of weight is the gram. It is much smaller than the smallest commonly used unit of weight in the United States, the ounce. An ounce of capers is on the left, and a gram is on the right.

42

METRIC CONVERSION IN THE FOOD-SERVICE INDUSTRY

There are many metric measures. The conversions used most often in food service follow.

Weight (Mass)	Volume (Liquid)
1 gram = 1,000 milligrams 1,000 grams = 1 kilogram	1,000 milliliters = 1 liter

Weight Conversion between U.S. Standard Measure and Metric	Volume Conversion between U.S. Standard Measure and Metric
1 ounce = 28.35 grams 1 kilogram = 2.21 pounds	1 liter = 33.8 fluid ounces

When you have committed to memory the above metric facts, the measurement facts in Chapter 2 (page 25), and the conversion methods used in Chapters 4 (pages 51 and 54) and 5 (page 61), you will be able to convert any quantity you may need to use in the kitchen between metric and U.S. standard measures.

USING METRIC MEASURE

When using the metric system, keep in mind that only liquids are measured by liters or milliliters (volume). Grams, milligrams, and kilograms, on the other hand, measure solids (weight). If you were working in a kitchen in Europe and you had a recipe from the United States, you might want to convert it to metric measures so that your co-workers could understand the recipe. For instance, the recipe for New England Clam Chowder that you want to use requires some of the following ingredients:

- 4 pounds potatoes

- 1 teaspoon salt

- 6 quarts fish stock

- 10 ounces minced onion

- 1 teaspoon hot pepper sauce

The following table describes the best unit of metric measure for each of the above ingredients.

43

Examples of Measuring Metric		
Unit Used in U.S. Standard Measure	**Metric Measure Unit**	**Reasoning**
Pounds of potatoes	kilogram	Solids are measured in grams; because this is a large quantity, kilograms would be appropriate.
Teaspoons of salt	gram	This is a small quantity of a solid and should therefore be measured in grams.
Quarts of fish stock	liter	Liquids are measured in liters.
Ounces of minced onions	gram	Solids are measured in grams.
Teaspoons of hot pepper sauce	milliliter	The pepper sauce is a liquid, so it should be measured in liters. Since it is such a small quantity, milliliters would be best.

See Chapter 5, page 60, for actual conversion techniques for these ingredients.

CHAPTER REVIEW

Being familiar with metric units of measure that are commonly used in the kitchen is imperative for success in the food-service industry. Your knowledge of the metric measure will prevent many mistakes in cooking and in purchasing.

Weight (Mass)	**Volume (Liquid)**
1 gram = 1,000 milligrams 1,000 grams = 1 kilogram	1,000 milliliters = 1 liter

Weight Conversion between U.S. Standard Measure and Metric	**Volume Conversion between U.S. Standard Measure and Metric**
1 ounce = 28.35 grams 1 kilogram = 2.21 pounds	1 liter = 33.8 fluid ounces

In the introduction to this chapter there is a scenario describing the need for 100 grams of butter from the walk-in. Now you can see that if 1 ounce is equal to 28.35 grams, 100 grams would be only a few ounces of butter. Three cases of butter would be thousands of grams beyond what you needed, and a good reason for the chef to laugh. The metric system is slowly but surely making its way into the U.S. market. The more prepared you are, the easier that transition will be for you and your kitchen.

STUDY AIDS

Make flash cards using index cards or small pieces of paper and the table below to assist you.

MEASUREMENT STUDY CARDS	
Front of the Card	**Back of the Card**
1 gram = _____ milligram(s)	1 gram = __1,000__ milligram(s)
1,000 grams = _____ kilogram(s)	1,000 grams = ___1___ kilogram(s)
1 ounce = _____ gram(s)	1 ounce = __28.35__ gram(s)
1 kilogram = _____ pound(s)	1 kilogram = __2.21__ pound(s)
1 liter = _____ fluid ounce(s)	1 liter = __33.8__ fluid ounce(s)
1,000 milliliters = _____ liter(s)	1,000 milliliters = ___1___ liter(s)
1,000 liters = _____ kiloliter(s)	1,000 liters = ___1___ kiloliter(s)

CHAPTER PRACTICE

Answers to odd-numbered questions may be found on page 251.

1. One liter is equal to _____ fluid ounce(s).

2. Which is heavier: 1 ounce of parsley or 1 gram of parsley?

_____

_____

_____

_____

_____

3. Which holds more orange juice: 1 liter or 1 quart?

_____

_____

_____

_____

_____

45

4. One gram is what percent of 1 ounce? Round your answer to the nearest tenth percent.

_____

_____

_____

_____

_____

5. One cup of rice wine vinegar is what percent of 1 liter? Round your answer to the nearest tenth percent.

_____

_____

_____

_____

_____

6. Name three reasons why it is important to know the metric system in the food-service industry.

_____

_____

_____

_____

_____

7. Which is heavier: 3 pounds of flour or 3 kilograms of flour?

_____

_____

_____

_____

_____

8. Which is smaller: a liter or 3 pints?

_____

_____

_____

_____

_____

9. Name something that you think weighs about 1 gram.

_____

_____

_____

_____

_____

10. Name a unit of U.S. standard measure that contains about 1 liter.

_____

_____

_____

_____

_____

11. What percent of a cup is 7 tablespoons?

_____

_____

_____

_____

_____

12. What percent of a quart is $\frac{1}{2}$ cup?

_____

_____

_____

_____

_____

13. One-half cup of water equals _____ fluid ounce(s).

14. Ten fluid ounces is what percent of 1 pint?

_____

_____

_____

_____

_____

47

15. Which is heavier: 1 kilogram or 5 cups of water?

_____

_____

_____

_____

16. One gram is what percent of 1 kilogram?

_____

_____

_____

_____

17. One milliliter is what percent of 1 liter?

_____

_____

_____

_____

Test yourself. In one minute or less, complete the following:

18. 1 ounce = _____ gram(s)

19. 1 liter = _____ fluid ounce(s)

20. 1 kilogram = _____ pound(s)

21. 1 liter = _____ milliliter(s)

22. 1 kilogram = _____ gram(s)

23. What would be the appropriate metric unit of measurement for the following ingredient quantities: kilogram, gram, liter, or milliliter?

Ingredient in U.S. Standard Measure	Best Metric Measure
10-pound bag of sugar	
¼ teaspoon of salt	
1½ cups of olive oil	
10 ounces of flour	
2 tablespoons of milk	

Basic Conversion of Units of Measure within Volume or Weight

4

You are making vegetable burgers, and the recipe calls for 36 ounces of ground walnuts. Walnuts are only available from your supplier in pound units. You must be able to calculate that $2\frac{1}{4}$ pounds is equivalent to 36 ounces so that you can place your order. Once you understand the units of measure and how they are related, you will be able to convert easily from one to the other. In the food-service industry, units of measure are how we communicate quantities of food and beverages.

It is common to purchase a product in pounds and use it in ounces or grams, or to purchase in liters and use it in fluid ounces. In this chapter, we are going to investigate converting units of measure within volume or within weight. In the next chapter, we will convert volume to weight measures and weight to volume measures.

OBJECTIVES

- Demonstrate your understanding of the bridge method to convert units of measure within weight.

- Demonstrate your understanding of the bridge method to convert units of measure within volume.

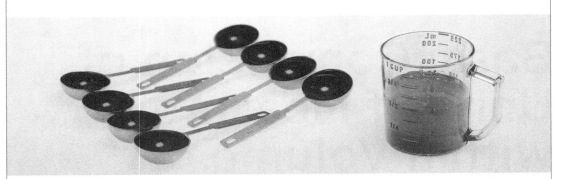

If you were quadrupling a recipe that called for 2 tablespoons of honey, it would be much more difficult and less accurate to measure 8 tablespoons rather than its equivalent, ½ cup.

CONVERTING UNITS OF MEASURE: THE BASICS

How would a calculation such as converting 36 ounces to 2 ¼ pounds be done?

The *bridge method* is the "recipe" for converting one unit of measure to another. It can be used to make conversations in these circumstances:

- Within U.S. standard weight and volume measures, ounces can be converted to pounds, quarts to pints, tablespoons to cups.

- Within metric weight and volume measures, liters can be converted to milliliters, grams to kilograms.

- Between metric measures and U.S. standard measures, grams can be converted to ounces, fluid ounces to liters.

- Between weight and volume (see Chapter 6, page 71), pounds can be converted to cups, grams to teaspoons.

The bridge method is not the only method that can be used to make unit conversions. An alternative method or shortcut will be discussed at the end of this chapter.

The following tables for the weight and volume equivalents from Chapters 2 and 3 have been provided for easy reference below.

U.S. STANDARD VOLUME EQUIVALENTS	
Volume Measures	**Volume Equivalents**
1 tablespoon	3 teaspoons
1 cup	16 tablespoons
1 pint	2 cups
1 quart	2 pints
1 gallon	4 quarts

U.S. STANDARD WEIGHT EQUIVALENT		
	1 pound = 16 ounces	

METRIC VOLUME AND WEIGHT EQUIVALENTS

Weight (Mass)	Liquid (Volume)	
1 gram = 1,000 milligrams	1 liter = 33.8 fluid ounces	
1,000 grams = 1 kilogram	1,000 milliliters = 1 liter	
1 ounce = 28.35 grams	1,000 liters = 1 kiloliter	
1 kilogram = 2.21 pounds		

BRIDGE METHOD: A RECIPE FOR CONVERSION

INGREDIENTS

- Unit of measurement to be converted

- Unit of measurement to be converted to

- Equivalencies from Chapters 2 and 3

STEPS FOR THE BRIDGE METHOD

STEP 1. If the unit of measurement that you are converting is a whole number, put it over 1. If it is a fraction, first convert it to a decimal and then put it over 1.

STEP 2. Place a multiplication sign next to this.

STEP 3. Draw another fraction line.

STEP 4. Put in the units of measurement. The unit of measurement to be removed is written on the bottom. The unit of measurement being converted to is written on the top.

STEP 5. Enter the numbers to create the equivalency.

STEP 6. Multiply straight across, disregarding the different units of measurement.

STEP 7. Reduce the resulting fraction (if necessary).

STEP 8. Cancel like units of measurement and carry over the remaining unit of measurement to the answer.

NOTE

Occasionally there will be slight variations in answers dealing with weight in metric form. This variation is caused by the common equivalency: 1 kilogram = 2.21 pounds. The pound equivalent for 1 kilogram has been rounded from 2.2045. This difference can create a discrepancy in answers generated by using the 1 ounce = 28.35 conversion. None of the answers are wrong based on the conversion difference, but they may appear that way. When examining answers that look slightly different, it is a good idea to look back at the work to check if the conversions are the cause of the different outcomes. Additionally, for the purposes of this math text, these differences are fine. When you are working in the food-service industry, you will need to decide how accurate you want to be and, as a result, use the appropriate numbers based on that decision.

STEPS TO CONVERTING UNITS OF MEASURE USING THE BRIDGE METHOD

EXAMPLE 1:

Convert 36 ounces to pounds.

STEP 1. If the number in the unit of measurement that you are converting is a whole number, put it over 1. If it is a fraction, first convert it to a decimal and then put it over 1.

$$\frac{36 \text{ oz}}{1}$$

STEP 2. Place a multiplication sign next to this.

$$\frac{36 \text{ oz}}{1} \times$$

STEP 3. Draw another fraction line.

$$\frac{36 \text{ oz}}{1} \times \underline{\hspace{2cm}}$$

STEP 4. Put in the units of measurement. The unit of measurement to be removed (ounces) is written on the bottom. The unit of measurement being converted to (pounds) is written on top.

$$\frac{36 \text{ oz}}{1} \times \frac{\text{lb}}{\text{oz}}$$

STEP 5. Enter the numbers to create the equivalency (1 pound = 16 ounces).

$$\frac{36 \text{ oz}}{1} \times \frac{1 \text{ lb}}{16 \text{ oz}}$$

STEP 6. Multiply straight across. Disregard the different units of measurement.

$$\frac{36 \text{ oz}}{1} \times \frac{1 \text{ lb}}{16 \text{ oz}} = \frac{36}{16}$$

STEP 7. Reduce the fraction answer if necessary.

$$\frac{36 \text{ oz}}{1} \times \frac{1 \text{ lb}}{16 \text{ oz}} = \frac{36}{16} = \frac{9}{4} = 2.25, \text{ or } 2\frac{1}{4}$$

STEP 8. Cancel like units of measurement and carry over the remaining unit of measurement to the answer.

$$\frac{36 \cancel{\text{ oz}}}{1} \times \frac{1 \text{ lb}}{16 \cancel{\text{ oz}}} = \frac{36}{16} = \frac{9}{4} = 2.25, \text{ or } 2\frac{1}{4} \text{ lb}$$

EXAMPLE 2:

Convert 12 teaspoons to cups. If you do not know the direct conversion from teaspoons to cups, you can go one step at a time and convert what you know.

STEP 1. Convert teaspoons to tablespoons.

$$\frac{12 \cancel{\text{ tsp}}}{1} \times \frac{1 \text{ tbsp}}{3 \cancel{\text{ tsp}}} = \frac{12}{3} = 4 \text{ tbsp}$$

STEP 2. Convert tablespoons to cups.

$$\frac{12 \cancel{\text{ tsp}}}{1} \times \frac{1 \text{ tbsp}}{3 \cancel{\text{ tsp}}} = \frac{12}{3} = 4 \text{ tbsp}$$

$$\frac{4 \cancel{\text{ tbsp}}}{1} \times \frac{1 \text{ cup}}{16 \cancel{\text{ tbsp}}} = \frac{4}{16} = 0.25 \text{ cup or } \frac{1}{4} \text{ cup}$$

The calculations indicate that 12 teaspoons is equal to ¼ cup. If you know there are 48 teaspoons in a cup, the conversation can be done more directly:

$$\frac{12 \cancel{\text{ tsp}}}{1} \times \frac{1 \text{ cup}}{48 \cancel{\text{ tsp}}} = \frac{12}{48} = 0.25 \text{ cup or } \frac{1}{4} \text{ cup}$$

The conversion may be done either way, and the results will be the same.

The bridge method may also be used to convert between U.S. standard measure and metric measure.

53

How many ounces are in 100 grams of butter?

$$\frac{100 \,\text{g}}{1} \times \frac{1 \text{ oz}}{28.35 \,\text{g}} = \frac{100}{28.35} = 3.5273 \text{ oz}$$

EXAMPLE 4:

A gallon of water is equivalent to how many liters?

$$\frac{1 \,\text{gal}}{1} \times \frac{128 \text{ fl oz}}{1 \,\text{gal}} = \frac{128 \,\text{fl oz}}{1} \times \frac{1 \text{ L}}{33.8 \,\text{fl oz}} = \frac{128}{33.8} = 3.7869 \text{ L}$$

THE ALTERNATE METHOD

Some people find the bridge method cumbersome and get frustrated with it. However, once it is mastered, any conversion calculation can be done with confidence. Eventually you will be able to solve problems dealing with conversions without the formality of writing down the steps. It is similar to what happens when you have made a recipe many times—eventually you no longer have to look at that recipe for direction because you have memorized it.

EXAMPLE:

Convert 66 ounces to pounds.

Bridge Method

$$\frac{66 \,\text{oz}}{1} \times \frac{1 \text{ lb}}{16 \,\text{oz}} = \frac{66}{16} = 4.125 \text{ lb or } 4\frac{1}{8} \text{ lb}$$

A Shortcut

Some people are able to see the 66 ounces and know to divide by 16:

$$\frac{66}{16} = 4.125 \text{ lb or } 4\frac{1}{8} \text{ lb}$$

Be careful doing calculations using the shortcut because it is very easy to perform the wrong operations and end up with the wrong answer. In the kitchen, wrong answers can be costly and time-consuming. For instance, many times students will *multiply* 66 by 16 and end up with 1,056 lb—though if you take the time to determine if the answer is reasonable, as suggested in Chapter 1, page 1, you will see that this cannot be right.

CHAPTER REVIEW

In this chapter, we discussed two methods of converting units of measure.

- The bridge method has three key ingredients: units of measurement to be converted, units of measurement being converted to, and equivalencies (from Chapters 2, page 30, and 3, page 40).

    STEP 1. If the unit of measurement that you are converting is a whole number, put it over 1. If it is a fraction, first convert it to a decimal and then put it over 1.

    STEP 2. Place a multiplication sign next to this.

    STEP 3. Draw another fraction line.

    STEP 4. Put in the units of measurement. The unit of measurement to be removed is written on the bottom. The unit of measurement being converted to is written on the top.

    STEP 5. Enter the numbers to create the equivalency.

    STEP 6. Multiply straight across, disregarding the different units of measurement.

    STEP 7. Reduce the resulting fraction (if necessary).

    STEP 8. Cancel like units of measurement and carry over the remaining unit of measurement to the answer.

- The alternate method is essentially the bridge method without writing all the steps down. This route is good for the expert converter, but for a novice it can lead to mistakes.

CHAPTER PRACTICE

Answers to odd-numbered questions may be found on page 251.

1. A bag of alfalfa sprouts contains 1 pound. How many grams of alfalfa do you have?

_____

_____

_____

_____

_____

55

2. You purchase a bottle of pomegranate syrup that contains 12 fluid ounces. How many tablespoons of pomegranate syrup do you have?

_____

_____

_____

_____

_____

3. One teaspoon is equal to _____ fluid ounces.

4. Three-quarters cup is equal to _____ fluid ounces.

5. You have just converted a recipe that now calls for 128 teaspoons of butter. How many cups of butter should you use?

_____

_____

_____

_____

_____

Convert the following using the bridge method. Leave your answers in decimal form. Final answers should be truncated at the ten-thousandths place value (for example, 10.456789 should be left as 10.4567).

6. 13# = _____ oz

7. 3.5 gallons = _____ qt

8. 0.875 pint = _____ cup(s)

9. 24 tsp = _____ cup(s)

10. 9 cups = _____ quart(s)

11. 76 oz = _____ #

12. $\frac{1}{3}$ cup = _____ tbsp

13. 32 tbsp = _____ cup(s)

14. 14 tsp = _____ tbsp

15. 2.5 kg = _____ g

16. 1,750 mL = _____ L

17. 75 fl oz = _____ gallon(s)

18. 55 tsp = _____ cup(s)

19. 52 cups = _____ quart(s)

20. $3\frac{1}{2}$ quart = _____ pint(s)

21. 4.0325# = _____ oz

22. $1\frac{1}{2}$ pints = _____ tbsp

23. $\frac{1}{3}$ quart = _____ fl oz

24. 10 quarts = _____ gallon(s)

25. $\frac{1}{4}$ cup = _____ tsp

26. 4 pints = _____ quart(s)

27. $\frac{2}{3}$ cup = _____ tsp

28. 18 tsp = _____ cup(s)

29. $\frac{1}{4}$ qt = _____ gallon(s)

30. 26 tbsp = _____ cup(s)

31. 105 tbsp = _____ qt

32. 6 oz = _____ gram(s)

33. 600 grams = _____ pound(s)

34. 8.5 qt = _____ gallon(s)

35. $\frac{1}{8}$ pint = _____ tbsp

36. $\frac{1}{3}$ cup = _____ tsp

37. 11 oz = _____ #

38. 210 cups = _____ gallon(s)

39. $5\frac{1}{3}$ fl oz = _____ pints

40. 11 tbsp = _____ tsp

41. $\frac{3}{10}$ oz = _____ #

42. $\frac{3}{4}$ pint = _____ fl oz

43. $\frac{3}{4}$ cup = _____ tbsp

44. 0.25# = _____ oz

45. 75 mL = _____ fl oz

46. 9 tbsp = _____ tsp

47. $\frac{7}{10}$ cup = _____ tbsp

48. $\frac{3}{4}$ oz = _____ gram(s)

Use the bridge method to solve the following word problems.

49. How many ounces are in 1 kilogram?

_____

_____

_____

_____

_____

50. How many pounds of flour are in a 10-kilogram bag of flour?

_____

_____

_____

_____

_____

51. You are making 10 cakes. Each cake will contain 6 ounces of ground pecans. How many kilograms of pecans will you need?

_____

_____

_____

_____

_____

52. If 1 chicken weighs 4.5 pounds, how many kilograms do 3 chickens weigh?

_____

_____

_____

_____

_____

53. If a recipe calls for 1,140 grams of chocolate, how many pounds do you need to order?

_____

_____

_____

_____

_____

Converting Weight and Volume Mixed Measures

5

Y ou will be using a recipe that calls for 2 pounds 12 ounces of sugar. Sugar is purchased by the pound, so this quantity must be converted to 2.75 pounds for you to place the order. Converting to and from mixed measures will help in preparing, costing, and ordering ingredients for a recipe.

Converting single units of measure to mixed units of measure will help in the physical measuring of ingredients by saving time and reducing the chance for error. Imagine you had to increase the yield of a recipe for Hot and Spicy Eggplant to meet your needs. Originally, the recipe called for 1 tablespoon of chopped scallions. After you convert the recipe, it now calls for 18 tablespoons of chopped scallions. In this instance, it is more reasonable to convert the 18 tablespoons to a mixed unit of measure, as it is more practical to measure 1 cup plus 2 tablespoons of chopped scallions than to measure out 18 tablespoons. Not only is it more practical, but also it is certainly a more reasonable measurement to hand over to your sous chef or print in a newspaper or magazine. It is considered more accurate, however, to weigh the scallions; in Chapter 6, page 71, the topic of converting volume to weight is covered.

OBJECTIVES

- Convert mixed units of measure to a single unit.

- Convert a single unit of measure to mixed units of measure.

USING THE BRIDGE METHOD

EXAMPLE 1:

The recipe in the chapter introduction called for 2 pounds 12 ounces of sugar. You purchase sugar by the pound and therefore need to convert this quantity so that it is all in pounds. In examining this mixed measure, you see that the 2 pounds is already in pounds, but the 12 ounces must be converted to pounds using the bridge method.

$$12 \text{ oz} = \frac{12 \text{ oz}}{1} \times \frac{1 \text{ lb}}{16 \text{ oz}} = \frac{12}{16} = 0.75 \text{ lb} + 2 \text{ lb} = 2.75 \text{ lb}$$

EXAMPLE 2:

You have converted the yield of a recipe, and it now calls for 18 tablespoons of chopped scallions. To save time and reduce the chance for error, you need to convert this to a larger unit of measure. Using the bridge method, the problem can be set up as follows:

$$\frac{18 \text{ tbsp}}{1} \times \frac{1 \text{ cup}}{16 \text{ tbsp}} = \frac{18}{16} = 1.125 \text{ cups}$$

It wouldn't be reasonable to ask someone to measure 1.125 cups. However, there are 16 tablespoons in 1 cup, and 16 divides evenly into 18 one time, with 2 left over. Therefore, 1.125 cups is equivalent to 1 cup plus 2 tablespoons.

EXAMPLE 3:

A recipe calls for 30 milliliters of vanilla. How many tablespoons do you need to use?
   The first step is to convert milliliters to fluid ounces.

$$\frac{30 \text{ mL}}{1} \times \frac{1 \text{ L}}{1000 \text{ mL}} = \frac{30}{1000} = 0.03 \text{ L}$$

$$\frac{0.03 \text{ L}}{1} \times \frac{33.8 \text{ fl oz}}{1 \text{ L}} = 1.014 \text{ fl oz}$$

Now that we have fluid ounces, we can convert to tablespoons.

$$\frac{1.014 \text{ fl oz}}{1} \times \frac{1 \text{ tbsp}}{0.5 \text{ fl oz}} = 2.028 \text{ tbsp}$$

EXAMPLE 4:

Problem 30 from the end of Chapter 4 reads as follows:

26 tbsp = _____ cup(s)

You should have gotten 1.625 cups as an answer. If you need to measure this amount, it would be more helpful to convert the 0.625 to an easily measurable quantity.

The first step is to convert tablespoons to cups:

$$\frac{26 \ \text{tbsp}}{1} \times \frac{1 \ \text{cup}}{16 \ \text{tbsp}} = \frac{26}{16} = 1.625 \ \text{cups}$$

$$\frac{0.625 \ \text{cup}}{1} \times \frac{16 \ \text{tbsp}}{1 \ \text{cup}} = 10 \ \text{tbsp}$$

Thus, 1.625 cups is equal to 1 cup plus 10 tablespoons. However, measuring out 10 tablespoons could take a lot of time and increases the possibility of error. Is there a better way to measure 10 tablespoons? Consider that 8 tablespoons is equal to $\frac{1}{2}$ cup. Subtract 8 tablespoons from 10 tablespoons, and there are 2 tablespoons remaining. So an easy way to write 1.625 cups is $1\frac{1}{2}$ cups plus 2 tablespoons.

With this type of conversion, there will be more than one correct answer. For instance, a recipe might call for 3 pounds 4 ounces, 3.25 pounds, 52 ounces, or 1.47 kilograms of sugar; all of these amounts are the same, only expressed in different units. Each unit of measure might be best suited for one particular application:

- The 3-pound 4-ounce measure of sugar might be preferred for weighing out mise en place instead of 3.25 pounds if you are not working with a digital scale.

- The pound measure might be necessary for ordering, as many items such as sugar are sold by the pound.

- The ounce measurement might be the easiest to use for costing if the price per ounce is known. An example of this would be most spices.

- The metric measurement might be the choice when you work in an establishment that uses the metric system.

CHAPTER REVIEW

Converting units of measure to more reasonable quantities is an important skill with which all professional chefs should be proficient. Much time and money may be wasted when poor measurement quantities are used. Knowing the weight and volume equivalents is critical for the successful application of this math.

Important concepts to remember when converting units of measure:

- The bridge method helps you keep track of the units while doing the correct math.

- There is always more than one way to express a unit of measure.

- Adjusting measures to more reasonable units will save time and prevent errors.

- Be careful about rounding! If you convert a mixed unit of measure to 1.89 cups, it is not always a good idea to round that to 2 cups.

CHAPTER PRACTICE

Answers to odd-numbered questions may be found on page 251.

Convert each given measurement to the unit stated directly above. Show all work. Leave your answers in decimal form. Final answers should be truncated at the ten-thousandths place value (for example, 10.456789 should be left as 10.4567).

1. Represent in kilograms:

    A. 5# 11 oz

    B. 6.25 #

    C. 8# 6 oz

    D. 115 oz

2. Represent in an appropriate volume measure, such as tsp, tbsp, cup, pints, quarts, gallons:

    A. 10 fl oz

    B. $\frac{1}{2}$ fl oz

    C. 256 fl oz

    D. 20 fl oz

3. Represent in liters:

    A. 16 quarts 3 tablespoons

    B. 1 quart 2 pints

    C. 1 gallon

    D. $\frac{1}{2}$ cup

4. Represent in pounds:

    A. 20# 9 oz

    B. 3# 3 oz

    C. 110# 14 oz

    D. 12# 1 oz

5. Represent in quarts:

  A. 3 quarts 4 cups

  B. 0.25 gallons 3 cups

  C. $8\dfrac{3}{4}$ pints $5\dfrac{1}{2}$ cups

  D. 12 quarts 12 tablespoons

6. Represent in pints:

  A. 4 pints 3 quarts

  B. 2 pints 1 gallon

  C. $\dfrac{3}{4}$ pint 3 cups

  D. 750 milliliters

7. Represent in ounces:

  A. 28#

  B. 0.375#

  C. 2# 9 oz

  D. 750 grams

8. Represent in cups:

  A. 1 quart 4 pints

  B. 14 teaspoons

  C. $2\dfrac{1}{2}$ liters

  D. 48 tablespoons

9. Represent in gallons:

  A. 8 qt 10 pt

  B. 3 pt 108 tbsp

  C. 7 gal 120 qt

  D. 52 cups

10. Represent in tablespoons:

A. $\dfrac{3}{4}$ cup

B. $\dfrac{1}{8}$ pint

C. 18 teaspoons

D. 0.0625 cup

11. Represent in teaspoons:

A. $\dfrac{1}{14}$ cup

B. 0.0123 pint

C. 1.5 tablespoons

D. 0.125 cup

12. Represent in grams:

A. $1\dfrac{1}{2}$ kilograms

B. 0.33 kilogram

C. 1 pound

D. 3 ounces

Use the following information to answer Questions 13 and 14.

You purchase 3 bunches of beets. Each bunch weighs 2 pounds 9 ounces.

13. How many pounds of beets do you have?

_____

_____

_____

_____

_____

14. How many grams of beets do you have?

_____

_____

_____

_____

_____

15. You receive a case of tomato juice. Each case contains four 1-gallon containers of juice. If you serve fifteen 4-fluid-ounce portions of the juice, what percent of the juice will be *left over?*

_____

_____

_____

_____

_____

16. You are preparing tarts. Each tart shell consists of 3 ounces of flour. If you prepare 40 tarts, how many pounds of flour do you need?

_____

_____

_____

_____

_____

17. A recipe calls for ⅔ cup of milk. You wish to make half of the recipe. How many tablespoons of milk should you use?

_____

_____

_____

_____

_____

18. You have a case of green beans, which weighs 25 pounds. You clean and trim the beans, and 22 pounds 6 ounces of the beans remains. What percent of the original 25 pounds of beans is clean?

_____

_____

_____

_____

_____

19. After increasing the yield of a recipe for soup, you have 147 cups of water. What would be a better way of measuring this amount?

_____

_____

_____

_____

_____

20. A bag of flour has 42 pounds 8 ounces remaining in it. You estimate that you have used 15 percent of the flour. How many pounds of flour did the bag originally hold?

_____

_____

_____

_____

21. You have 29 teaspoons. What percent of a cup does this represent?

_____

_____

_____

_____

_____

22. Forty fluid ounces of water is equivalent to _____ quart(s).

23. You are serving 3-ounce portions of fruit salad. How many _full_ portions can be obtained from 7 pounds 10 ounces of fruit salad?

_____

_____

_____

_____

_____

24. Three tablespoons is equivalent to what percent of a liter?

_____

_____

_____

_____

_____

25. You need 5 pounds 6 ounces of imported cheese. How many _full_ kilograms of cheese should you order?

_____

_____

_____

_____

_____

26. You need to increase a recipe by 40 percent. The original recipe calls for 1 ½ pints of cream. How many pints of cream should you use to make the new recipe?

_____

_____

_____

_____

_____

27. Represent 3.125 pounds in two other ways.

_____

_____

_____

_____

_____

28. Represent 9 cups in quarts.

_____

_____

_____

_____

_____

29. Represent 0.046875 quart in tablespoons.

_____

_____

_____

_____

_____

30. Represent 0.8333 tablespoons in teaspoons.

_____

_____

_____

_____

_____

31. You have 2 pounds 12 ounces of cheddar cheese. The recipe calls for 1.75 kilograms of grated cheddar cheese. Will you have enough cheese to make this recipe?

_____

_____

_____

_____

_____

32. A recipe calls for 50 mL of oil. How many tablespoons is this?

_____

_____

_____

_____

_____

33. You increase a recipe by 30 percent. The original recipe calls for 2 cups of diced carrots. How many cups of carrots will the new recipe require?

_____

_____

_____

_____

_____

34. After converting a recipe's size you need 0.125 quart of milk. What would be a better way of measuring that amount?

_____

_____

_____

_____

_____

35. Which weighs more: 2.21 pounds or 2.21 kilograms?

_____

_____

_____

_____

_____

Advanced Conversions between Weight and Volume

6

You have been hired to cater a party and are calculating the cost of the food. One of the dishes you will be preparing is green beans with walnuts. The recipe calls for 1 ½ cups of walnuts. In order to calculate the amount to charge for the dish, you need to determine the cost of each ingredient. You look up walnuts on the invoice from the purveyor and find that they are sold by the pound, not by the cup. Pounds are a unit of weight, while cups are a unit of volume. To figure out the cost, you need to convert the cups of walnuts into pounds.

At the end of the party, one of the guests asks for your recipe for carrot cake, which you also prepared for the party. The carrot cake recipe calls for 1 ¼ pounds of all-purpose flour. Most people do not have a kitchen scale and are not familiar with weighing ingredients for baking or cooking. You want to convert the weight unit into a volume unit with which the guest will be more familiar.

In this chapter, we will examine how to solve problems such as these using the Approximate Volume to Weight Chart, page 74. Over the course of your career as a culinary professional you will encounter two different types of measure—volume and weight. It is essential that you understand the difference between these two types of measure so that you can work accurately and efficiently while converting between them. Errors with weight and volume can be costly and time-consuming. In order to prepare recipes, cost recipes, order ingredients, share recipes, publish recipes, and perform many other kitchen tasks, you will want to convert units of measure between weight and volume. As always, keep in mind that when converting, you must choose a measurement that makes sense in the situation.

APPROXIMATE EQUIVALENT OF FOOD MEASURES

When discussing the weight of foods in volume measures, it is good to start with water and fluid ounces. A fluid ounce is a volume measure that is based on the amount of space filled by 1 ounce of water. The chart below lists the volume equivalents for fluid ounces from Chapter 2, page 30.

ADDITIONAL VOLUME EQUIVALENTS

Volume Measure	Equivalent in Fluid Ounces
1 tablespoon	1/2 fluid ounce
1 cup	8 fluid ounces
1 pint	16 fluid ounces
1 quart	32 fluid ounces
1 gallon	128 fluid ounces

If an ingredient other than water is measured in a cup, then it is *not* safe to assume that it weighs 8 ounces. You cannot assume that any other substance has the same density as water and weighs the same as water or water-like liquids in a given volume measure.

If you fill a measuring cup with honey and place it on a scale, it will not weigh 8 ounces (as water would); it will weigh 12 ounces because honey is heavier (denser) than water. When something other than water is measured by volume, it is a common mistake to assume that "a pint is a pound the world round." If you are dealing with something other than water or a water-like liquid, you have two choices: weigh the measured volume of the ingredient, or use the Approximate Volume to Weight Chart provided in this chapter to calculate the conversion. Although it might be more convenient to use a chart to make the calculation, be aware that any information in this chart—or any chart such as this—is an approximation, and if accuracy is important, the desired amount of the ingredient should be weighed.

1 cup, or 8 fluid ounces, of honey does not weigh 8 ounces—it weighs 12 ounces.

INTRODUCTION TO THE APPROXIMATE VOLUME TO WEIGHT CHART

The following chart provides information for converting between volume and weight measures. The first column lists the item. The second column gives a volume measure: tablespoon (T), cup (C), quart (qt), or each (ea). The last column gives the approximate weight, in ounces, of the given volume measure for that particular item.

Let's take a look at how the information in the chart is laid out.

Ingredient	Volume	Ounces

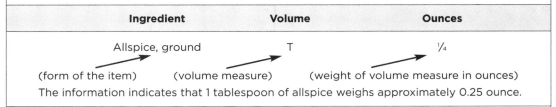

| Allspice, ground | T | ¼ |
| (form of the item) | (volume measure) | (weight of volume measure in ounces) |

The information indicates that 1 tablespoon of allspice weighs approximately 0.25 ounce.

Information for the following Approximate Volume to Weight Chart was gathered by simply weighing the listed fabricated and nonfabricated foods in cups and tablespoons. You could create your own chart of the foods you use commonly in your kitchen that are not on this list. It is very important to measure and weigh with accuracy and consistency. Small mistakes could result in large errors when applied to substantial quantities. You might also want to create a chart of metric conversions from cups and tablespoons.

APPROXIMATE VOLUME TO WEIGHT CHART

Ingredient	Volume	Ounces	Ingredient	Volume	Ounces
Allspice, ground	T	$\frac{1}{4}$	Cake crumbs, soft	C	$2\frac{3}{4}$
Almonds, blanched	C	$5\frac{1}{3}$	Carrots, raw or cooked, diced	C	$5\frac{1}{3}$
Apples			Celery, diced†	C	4
peeled, $\frac{1}{2}$ in cubes	C	$3\frac{1}{3}$	Celery seed	T	$\frac{1}{4}$
pie, canned	C	6	Cheese		
sauce, canned	C	8	cottage or cream	C	8
Apricots			grated, hard (e.g., parmesan)	C	4
drained, canned	C	$5\frac{1}{3}$	grated, medium (e.g., cheddar)	C	3
halves, dried	C	$4\frac{1}{2}$	grated, soft (e.g., fresh goat)	C	$4\frac{3}{4}$
Asparagus†	C	$6\frac{1}{2}$	Cherries, glacéed	C	$6\frac{1}{2}$
Baking powder	T	$\frac{1}{2}$	Chicken, cooked, cubed	C	$5\frac{1}{3}$
Bananas, diced	C	$6\frac{1}{2}$	Chili powder	T	$\frac{1}{4}$
Barley, raw	C	8	Chili sauce	C	$11\frac{1}{4}$
Beans			Chocolate		
baked	C	8	grated	C	$4\frac{1}{2}$
green†	C	$4\frac{1}{2}$	melted	C	8
kidney, dried	C	6	Cinnamon, ground	T	$\frac{1}{4}$
kidney, cooked	C	$6\frac{3}{4}$	Citron, dried, chopped	C	$6\frac{1}{2}$
lima, cooked	C	8	Cloves		
lima, dried	C	$6\frac{1}{2}$	ground	T	$\frac{1}{4}$
navy, dried	C	$6\frac{3}{4}$	whole	C	3
Bean sprouts	C	4	Cocoa	C	4
Beets, cooked, diced	C	$6\frac{1}{2}$	Coconut, shredded	C	$2\frac{1}{2}$
Blueberries			Corn, fresh, kernels†	C	$5\frac{3}{4}$
canned	C	$6\frac{1}{2}$	Corn flakes	C	1
fresh†	C	7	Cornmeal, raw	C	$5\frac{1}{3}$
Bread crumbs			Corn syrup	C	12
dried	C	4	Cornstarch	C	$4\frac{1}{2}$
soft	C	2	Cracker crumbs	C	3
Brussels sprouts	C	4	Cranberries		
Butter	C	8	raw	C	4
Cabbage, shredded†	C	4	sauce	C	8

*As-purchased quantity

†Edible portion quantity

(continues)

APPROXIMATE VOLUME TO WEIGHT CHART (Continued)

Ingredient	Volume	Ounces	Ingredient	Volume	Ounces
Cream			Mayonnaise	C	8
whipped	C	4	Milk		
whipping	C	8	condensed	C	$10\frac{2}{3}$
Cream of tartar	T	$\frac{1}{3}$	evaporated	C	9
Cream of wheat, raw	C	6	liquid	C	$8\frac{1}{2}$
Cucumbers, diced†	C	$5\frac{1}{3}$	nonfat dry	T	$\frac{1}{4}$
Currants, dried	C	$5\frac{1}{3}$	Mincemeat	C	8
Curry powder	T	$\frac{1}{4}$	Molasses	C	12
Dates, pitted	C	$6\frac{1}{5}$	Mustard		
Eggs			dry, ground	C	$3\frac{1}{2}$
dried, whites	C	$3\frac{1}{4}$	prepared	T	$\frac{1}{2}$
dried, yolks	C	$2\frac{3}{4}$	seed	T	$\frac{2}{5}$
fresh, whites (9)	C	8	Noodles, cooked	C	$5\frac{1}{3}$
fresh, yolks (10)	C	8	Nuts'	C	$4\frac{1}{2}$
raw, shelled (5 eggs)	C	8	Nutmeg, ground	T	$\frac{1}{4}$
Farina, raw	C	$5\frac{1}{3}$	Oil, vegetable	C	8
Figs, dried, chopped	C	$6\frac{1}{2}$	Onions, chopped	C	$6\frac{1}{2}$
Flour			Oysters, shucked	C	8
all-purpose	C	4	Paprika	T	$\frac{1}{4}$
bread, sifted	C	4	Parsley, coarsely chopped	C	1
bread, unsifted	C	$4\frac{1}{2}$	Peaches, chopped	C	8
cake or pastry, sifted	C	$3\frac{1}{3}$	Peanut butter	C	9
rye	C	$2\frac{3}{4}$	Peanuts†	C	5
soy	C	$3\frac{1}{4}$	Pears, fresh, diced†	C	$6\frac{1}{2}$
whole wheat	C	$4\frac{1}{4}$	Peas†	C	3.5
Gelatin, granulated	T	$\frac{1}{4}$	Pepper, ground	T	$\frac{1}{4}$
Ginger, ground	T	$\frac{1}{5}$	Peppers, green, chopped†	C	$5\frac{1}{3}$
Grapes			Pimiento, chopped	C	$6\frac{1}{2}$
cut, seeded	C	$5\frac{3}{4}$	Pineapple, crushed	C	8
whole†	C	4	Poppy seed	C	5
Ham, cooked, diced	C	$5\frac{1}{3}$	Potato chips	C	1
Honey	C	12	Potatoes, cooked, diced or mashed†	C	8
Horseradish	T	$\frac{1}{2}$	Prunes, dried	C	$6\frac{1}{2}$
Jam	C	12	Raisins	C	$5\frac{1}{3}$
Jelly	C	$10\frac{2}{3}$	Raisins, after cooking	C	7
Lard	C	8	Raspberries*	C	$4\frac{3}{4}$
Lettuce, shredded	C	$2\frac{1}{4}$	Rhubarb		
Margarine	C	8	cooked	C	$6\frac{1}{2}$
Marshmallows, large	80 ea	16	raw, 1 in dice	C	4

*As-purchased quantity

†Edible portion quantity

(continues)

Ingredient	Volume	Ounces	Ingredient	Volume	Ounces
Rice			Sugar		
cooked	C	8	brown, lightly packed	C	5⅓
uncooked	C	6.5	brown, solidly packed	C	8
Rutabaga, cubed	C	4¾	granulated	C	8
Sage, ground	C	2	powdered, sifted	C	5⅓
Salad dressing	C	8	Tapioca, pearl	C	5¾
Salmon, canned	C	8	Tea, loose-leaf	C	2⅔
Salt	T	⅔	Tomatoes		
Sauerkraut	C	5⅓	canned	C	8
Sesame seed	T	⅓	fresh, diced	C	7
Shallots, diced	T	⅖	Tuna	C	8
Shortening	C	7	Vanilla	T	½
Soda, baking	T	⅖	Vinegar	C	8
Spinach, raw†	qt	3¼	Walnuts, shelled	C	4
Squash, Hubbard, cooked	C	8	Water	C	8
Strawberries†	C	7	Yeast		
			compressed cake	ea	⅗
			envelope	ea	¼

*As-purchased quantity

†Edible portion quantity

STEPS TO SOLVING PROBLEMS USING THE APPROXIMATE VOLUME TO WEIGHT CHART

Whether you are dealing with a word problem in a culinary math class or in your kitchen, there are basic steps to follow to find the solution.

STEP 1. Determine whether you are converting from weight to volume or from volume to weight. Use the Approximate Volume to Weight Chart to find the ingredient's volume measure and its weight.

STEP 2. Convert the volume or weight of the ingredient that you want to convert to the unit used in the chart using the bridge method.

STEP 3. Using the bridge method, convert the ingredient to the desired weight or volume quantity.

EXAMPLE 1:

After increasing the yield of a recipe, it now calls for 24 tablespoons of walnuts. To determine the cost of the recipe, the weight equivalent of the walnuts in pounds must be calculated. The following steps demonstrate the method for making this conversion.

76

STEP 1. Use the Approximate Volume to Weight Chart to find the weight of walnuts. According to the chart, 1 cup of walnuts weighs 4 ounces.

STEP 2. Convert the 24 tablespoons to cups, because the chart gives the weight of 1 cup of walnuts, not 1 tablespoon. Use the bridge method to make this calculation.

$$\frac{24 \text{ tbsp}}{1} \times \frac{1 \text{ cup}}{16 \text{ tbsp}} = 1.5 \text{ cups}$$

STEP 3. Convert the cups to ounces, and the ounces to pounds.

$$\frac{1.5 \text{ cups}}{1} \times \frac{4 \text{ oz}}{1 \text{ cup}} = \frac{6 \text{ oz}}{1} \times \frac{1 \text{ lb}}{16 \text{ oz}} = 0.375 \text{ lb}$$

The calculations show that 24 tablespoons of walnuts is equivalent to 6 ounces, or 0.375 pound. The figure 0.375 pound might seem to be an awkward number to work with, but it is the number necessary to find the cost of the walnuts since they are purchased by the pound. (Finding cost will be covered in Chapter 9, page 120, and recipe costing in Chapter 11, page 154.)

EXAMPLE 2:

A recipe for carrot cake calls for 1 ¼ pounds of all-purpose flour. A customer requested this recipe, and as most people do not have a kitchen scale in their home, you would like to convert the 1 ¼ pounds of all-purpose flour into a cup measurement.

STEP 1. Consult the Approximate Volume to Weight Chart to find the weight of all-purpose flour. According to the chart, 1 cup of all-purpose flour weighs 4 ounces.

STEP 2. Convert the 1 ¼ pounds into ounces first, because the chart gives the weight of 1 cup of all-purpose flour in ounces, not in pounds. Use the bridge method to make this calculation.

$$\frac{1.25 \text{ lb}}{1} \times \frac{16 \text{ oz}}{1 \text{ lb}} = 20 \text{ oz}$$

STEP 3. Convert the ounces to cups.

$$\frac{20 \text{ oz}}{1} \times \frac{1 \text{ cup}}{4 \text{ oz}} = 5 \text{ cups}$$

EXAMPLE 3:

A recipe for Brandied Apricot Cake calls for 500 grams of dried apricots. A customer has requested this recipe. In the United States, most people are not very familiar with converting metric measure and do not have a metric scale. Therefore, you would want to convert the 500 grams of apricots into a cup measurement.

77

STEP 1. Consult the Approximate Volume to Weight Chart to find the weight of dried apricots. According to the chart, 1 cup of dried apricots weighs 4.5 ounces.

STEP 2. Convert the 500 grams into ounces first, because the chart gives the weight of 1 cup of apricots in ounces, not in grams. Use the bridge method to make this calculation.

$$\frac{500 \text{ g}}{1} \times \frac{1 \text{ oz}}{28.35 \text{ g}} = 17.6366 \text{ oz}$$

Since we are not finished calculating, we will carry this number four places past the decimal point.

STEP 3. Convert the ounces to cups.

$$\frac{17.6366 \text{ oz}}{1} \times \frac{1 \text{ cup}}{4.5 \text{ oz}} = 3.919 \text{ cups}$$

Because this is the end of our calculation you could round this number up to 4 cups. Since we are converting the amount of apricots and not baking powder, a leavening agent, the recipe will work. Having a few extra apricots will not noticeably affect the taste of the cake.

The calculations indicate that 500 grams of apricots are equivalent to approximately 4 cups.

EXAMPLE 4:

You have 100 grams of cinnamon. How many teaspoons of cinnamon do you have?

STEP 1. Use the Approximate Volume to Weight Chart to find the weight of cinnamon. According to the chart, 1 tablespoon of cinnamon weighs $\frac{1}{4}$ or 0.25 ounce.

STEP 2. Convert the 100 grams into ounces, because the chart gives the weight of 1 tablespoon of cinnamon in ounces, not grams. Use the bridge method to make this calculation.

$$\frac{100 \text{ g}}{1} \times \frac{1 \text{ oz}}{28.35 \text{ g}} = 3.5273 \text{ oz}$$

STEP 3. Convert the ounces to tablespoons, and then tablespoons to teaspoons.

$$\frac{3.5273 \text{ oz}}{1} \times \frac{1 \text{ tbsp}}{0.25 \text{ oz}} = \frac{14.1092 \text{ tbsp}}{1} \times \frac{3 \text{ tsp}}{1 \text{ tbsp}} = 42.3276 \text{ tsp, or } 42\frac{1}{3} \text{ tsp}$$

The result of the calculations indicates that 100 grams of cinnamon is equal to approximately 42 $\frac{1}{3}$ teaspoons of cinnamon. This would not be the best way to measure the cinnamon. You would probably want to convert to cups.

CHAPTER REVIEW

Converting between volume and weight is a skill that any professional chef needs to master in order to effectively manage the costs in a kitchen. Additionally, recipes that are used in a professional kitchen will need to be adjusted for the home cook or to produce a larger or smaller quantity of the recipe. When this is done, the ingredient's quantity will need to be altered, depending on the intended use of the recipe.

Follow the steps listed below to convert measurements using the Approximate Volume to Weight Chart, page 74.

STEP 1. Determine whether you are converting from weight to volume or from volume to weight. Use the Approximate Volume to Weight Chart to find the ingredient's volume measure and its weight.

STEP 2. Convert the volume or weight of the ingredient that you want to convert to the unit used in the chart using the bridge method.

STEP 3. Using the bridge method, convert the ingredient to the desired weight or volume quantity.

If you always keep in mind that all ingredients do not necessarily weigh 8 ounces in a cup, you can avoid many costly and time-wasting mistakes in the kitchen.

CHAPTER PRACTICE

Answers to odd-numbered questions may be found on page 251.

Find the answer to the following questions, using the Approximate Volume to Weight Chart on pages 74–76 if necessary. Leave your answers in decimal form. Final answers should be truncated at the ten-thousandths place value (for example, 10.456789 should be left as 10.4567).

1. A recipe calls for 5 ⅓ cups of dried bread crumbs. How many pounds of dried bread crumbs do you need to use?

_____

_____

_____

_____

_____

2. How many cups can be measured from 2 kilograms of honey?

_____

_____

_____

_____

_____

3. How many pounds of Parmesan cheese must you purchase in order to have 5 cups of grated cheese? _Hint:_ Look under "Cheese, grated" for the volume/weight conversion for Parmesan cheese.

_____

_____

_____

_____

_____

4. If a recipe calls for 2 gallons of fresh hulled strawberries, how many pounds should you use?

_____

_____

_____

_____

_____

5. How many ounces does 5 tablespoons of peanut butter weigh?

_____

_____

_____

_____

_____

6. How many tablespoons are in 1 pound of allspice?

_____

_____

_____

_____

_____

7. You need 6 cups of raw cream of wheat. How many 1-pound boxes of cream of wheat would you need to buy?

_____

_____

_____

_____

_____

8. A recipe for chocolate-coated almonds calls for 3 tablespoons of cocoa. How many ounces of cocoa should you use?

_____

_____

_____

_____

_____

9. How many pounds of mustard seed should you use if a recipe calls for $4\frac{1}{2}$ cups?

_____

_____

_____

_____

_____

10. How much would 1 teaspoon of cumin weigh if 1 cup of cumin weighs 4 ounces?

_____

_____

_____

_____

_____

11. How many tablespoons of salt are in a container of salt that weighs 1 pound 10 ounces?

_____

_____

_____

_____

_____

12. You are ordering ham for a breakfast you will be serving. You will be making omelets for 85 guests. Each omelet will need ¼ cup of cooked, diced ham. What is the minimum amount of ham, in pounds, that you should *order* to make the omelets?

_____

_____

_____

_____

_____

13. You have a container of chili powder that contains 1 pound 3 ounces. How many tablespoons will you be able to measure from the container?

_____

_____

_____

_____

_____

14. You have a banquet for 250 people. Dessert will be tapioca pudding. Your recipe calls for 1 cup of pearl tapioca for every 4 portions. How many pounds of pearl tapioca do you need to *purchase*?

_____

_____

_____

_____

_____

15. How much does 1 cup of cinnamon weigh in ounces?

_____

_____

_____

_____

16. How many grams of diced shallots are in 1 cup?

_____

_____

_____

_____

_____

82

17. You are making a dozen blueberry pies. The recipe for one pie calls for ³/₄ cup of granulated sugar. How many pounds of sugar do you need?

_____

_____

_____

_____

_____

18. A recipe calls for ³/₄ cup of dry raisins. If you are tripling the recipe, how many pounds of raisins should you use?

_____

_____

_____

_____

_____

19. After increasing a recipe, you determine that you will need 12 cups of whole wheat flour. How many pounds of whole wheat flour do you need to use?

_____

_____

_____

_____

_____

20. A recipe calls for 1 ¹/₂ quarts of dried lima beans. How many pounds should you add to the recipe?

_____

_____

_____

_____

_____

21. How many cups of rice can be measured from a 50-pound bag of rice?

_____

_____

_____

_____

_____

22. A recipe calls for 15 grams of granulated gelatin. How many teaspoons should you use?

_____

_____

_____

_____

_____

23. How many pints can be poured from a container with 2.5 kilograms of corn syrup?

_____

_____

_____

_____

_____

24. You have 5 kilograms of whole wheat flour. The recipe you are using calls for 4 cups of whole wheat flour and makes 10 servings. How many times can the recipe be made with the 5 kilograms of whole wheat flour?

_____

_____

_____

_____

_____

25. A recipe for Mango Tarte Tatin calls for 2 ½ teaspoons of fresh minced ginger. If 1 cup of fresh minced ginger weighs 4.5 ounces, then how many ounces of ginger will you need?

_____

_____

_____

_____

26. After cleaning and dicing potatoes, you have 3 ½ gallons of potatoes. If 1 cup of diced potatoes weighs 5 ounces, how many 4-ounce portions of cleaned diced potatoes could be obtained from the 3 ½ gallons of potatoes?

_____

_____

_____

_____

27. A recipe for chili yields 120 portions and calls for $8\frac{1}{2}$ pounds of fresh diced tomatoes. How many pints of tomatoes should you use?

_____

_____

_____

_____

_____

28. A recipe calls for 2 teaspoons of ground sage. How many ounces does 2 teaspoons of sage weigh?

_____

_____

_____

_____

_____

29. You are making prune coffee cake. The recipe makes one cake and calls for $2\frac{1}{2}$ cups of dried prunes. You want to make four cakes. How many pounds of prunes should you use for the four coffee cakes?

_____

_____

_____

_____

_____

30. You are making chocolate mousse pie. The recipe calls for $3\frac{1}{3}$ cups of grated chocolate. How many pounds of chocolate should you use?

_____

_____

_____

_____

_____

31. How many tablespoons of diced shallots can be measured from $\frac{3}{4}$ pound of diced shallots?

_____

_____

_____

_____

_____

32. You purchase a 5-pound sack of cornmeal. How many cups of cornmeal are in the sack?

_____

_____

_____

_____

_____

33. One cup of chopped peanuts weighs 5 ounces. How many ounces would 2 tablespoons plus 1 teaspoon weigh?

_____

_____

_____

_____

34. You are coating pans with bread crumbs. There are 30 pans to be coated, and each pan will need 2 tablespoons of dried bread crumbs. How many pounds of bread crumbs should you use?

_____

_____

_____

_____

35. A recipe calls for 12 ounces of molasses. The cook gets out a volume measuring container and measures out 12 fluid ounces of molasses.

A. What assumption did the cook make that was incorrect?

_____

_____

_____

_____

B. How much more molasses did the cook add than should have been added?

_____

_____

_____

_____

Yield Percent

7

Y ou are catering a party for 150 guests, and the food order must be in by noon today. One of the side dishes that you plan to serve is potatoes au gratin. You need 33 pounds 12 ounces of peeled, sliced potatoes for this recipe. Potatoes are ordered unpeeled; therefore, you will need a greater amount of unpeeled potatoes to yield enough peeled, sliced potatoes for the dish. If you purchased just 33 pounds 12 ounces of the unpeeled potatoes, there would not be enough to make the correct amount of potatoes au gratin for the event.

To get the desired weight of a cleaned and peeled product, the uncleaned and unpeeled weight of the product must be calculated. The factor used to make this calculation is called the yield percent.

Yield percent is commonly used in the kitchen to assist culinary professionals in determining amounts to order, recipe cost, and the number of servings that can be obtained from a given quantity. Understanding when to apply yield percent will help to avoid costly errors in over- or underordering, inaccuracies in costing, and shortfalls in available servings.

In addition, yield percent plays an important role in maintaining consistency in the kitchen. If a kitchen has a standard for the percent of a potato that is left after it is peeled, then the chef will be much more aware of any variations from that standard, thereby ensuring that there is no excessive waste.

- Calculate the yield percent of a nonfabricated fruit or vegetable, applying the steps of a yield test.

- Apply the terms *as-purchased quantity (APQ)*, *edible portion quantity (EPQ)*, and *trim* correctly.

- Calculate the yield percent when given the weights of the as-purchased quantity and edible portion quantity of a fruit or vegetable.

- Identify the factors that might affect yield percent.

- Distinguish the times when it is appropriate to use the Approximate Yield of Fruits and Vegetables Chart.

CHEF'S NOTE

Most professional recipes list ingredients and quantities in edible portion form. There are exceptions to this. For instance, a recipe might call for 1 pound of apples, sliced. Another recipe may call for 1 pound of sliced apples. There is a subtle difference in how these two recipes are written but a very big difference in what they mean. In the first recipe the word *sliced* follows the ingredient, which indicates that you should purchase 1 pound of apples and then prepare it. What you are left with (the prepared apples, less than a pound) is the amount that the recipe calls for. In the second example the recipe calls for 1 pound of sliced apples, which would indicate that you need to start with a greater quantity of apples, prepare it, and then have 1 pound remaining to be added to the recipe. It is important to be aware and read through the entire recipe directions to determine the form in which the ingredients are listed.

UNDERSTANDING AS-PURCHASED QUANTITY, EDIBLE PORTION QUANTITY, AND TRIM

AS-PURCHASED QUANTITY (APQ)

The *as-purchased quantity* is the weight, volume, or count of the nonfabricated fruit or vegetable. In other words, it is the quantity (weight, volume, or count) of the product as it is received from the vendor.

EDIBLE PORTION QUANTITY (EPQ)

The *edible portion quantity* is the weight, volume, or count of the fabricated fruit or vegetable. In other words, it is the quantity (weight, volume, or count) of the product after it has been

As-purchased whole pineapples, diced edible portion of the pineapples, and trim of the pineapples

cleaned, peeled, or prepared (fabricated) and is ready for use. The word *edible* in this term indicates the condition of the product as ready for use in preparing a dish. If you were to peel a 50-pound bag of potatoes, you would have a pile of cleaned potatoes ready to be used in a dish; this is the edible portion quantity (EPQ). The weight of these peeled potatoes should be approximately 42.5 pounds.

TRIM

Trim is the weight or volume of the waste. Trim, mathematically speaking, is the difference between APQ and EPQ:

APQ – EPQ = Trim

A 50-pound bag of potatoes yields approximately 42.5 pounds of cleaned, peeled potatoes, leaving approximately 7.5 pounds of trim (in this case, peels).

50 lb – 42.5 lb = 7.5 lb

Not all trim is loss or waste. Many say that if the trim is usable, then it is not waste. For instance, the potato peels may be used in a vegetable stock (though the value of those potato skins is so small it would not be worth allocating their cost to the soup in a cost determination—see

Chapter 10, page 138. Using the trim instead of throwing it away will make a kitchen run more cost-effectively. Whether and how the potato skins are used determines if the trim is loss or waste. However, in this model, all vegetable trim is assumed to be waste.

YIELD PERCENT

Yield percent is the percent of the as-purchased quantity that is edible.

There are three major applications for yield percent:

1. COMPUTING THE MINIMUM AMOUNT TO ORDER: For example, when the recipe calls for 3 pounds of peeled potatoes, the yield percent helps you to calculate the approximate minimum number of pounds of potatoes to order.

2. RECIPE COSTING: For example, when costing a recipe the yield percent can be used to adjust the cost of the 3 pounds of peeled potatoes to account for the fact that you had to purchase a quantity greater than the 3 pounds. This enables you to make sure that your selling price reflects the total cost for the potatoes.

3. DETERMINING THE MAXIMUM NUMBER OF SERVINGS THAT A PURCHASED AMOUNT WILL YIELD: For example, you purchase a 50-pound bag of potatoes. You can compute, using the yield percent, how many portions of mashed potatoes you can obtain from the 50-pound bag.

In this chapter, calculating yield percent will be the main objective. In later chapters these three applications of yield percent will be explored in greater detail.

The yield percent of a cantaloupe melon is 50 percent, which means that the edible portion quantity is one-half of the total as-purchased quantity.

THE MATH OF CALCULATING
YIELD PERCENT

YIELD PERCENT FORMULA

$$\text{Yield percent} = \frac{\text{Edible portion quantity}}{\text{As-purchased quantity}} \times 100$$

THE EPQ, APQ, AND YIELD PERCENT TRIANGLE

The following triangle is a tool used to find the yield percent, as-purchased quantity, and edible portion quantity. It is identical to the Percent Triangle introduced in Chapter 1, page 12, although the application differs.

PART = Edible portion quantity

WHOLE = As-purchased quantity

PERCENT = Yield percent

THE STEPS FOR USING THE EPQ, APQ, AND YIELD PERCENT TRIANGLE

STEP 1. Determine what you are looking for: EPQ, APQ, or yield percent.

STEP 2. *To find the edible portion quantity (EPQ)*
Cover the EPQ for edible portion quantity.

APQ and Y% are side by side. This directs you to multiply the APQ by the yield percent. (Remember to change the percent to a decimal by dividing by 100 before multiplying.)

To find the as-purchased quantity (APQ)
Cover the APQ for as-purchased quantity.

EPQ is over Y%. This directs you to divide the EPQ by the yield percent. (Remember to change the percent to a decimal by dividing by 100 before multiplying.)

To find the yield percent
Cover the Y% for yield percent.

EPQ is over APQ. This directs you to divide the EPQ by the APQ and multiply the answer by 100 to convert it to the yield percent.

STEPS FOR CALCULATING THE YIELD PERCENT

STEP 1. To calculate the yield percent for the potatoes, you must first identify the EPQ and the APQ.

91

STEP 2. Determine if the units are the same before calculating the yield percent. Use the bridge method (Chapter 4, page 50) if necessary.

STEP 3. Substitute the weights of the EPQ and APQ into the formula and solve.

EXAMPLE 1:

Fifty pounds of potatoes have been purchased. If the potatoes are weighed after cleaning and peeling, there will be approximately 42.5 pounds of cleaned potatoes and 7.5 pounds of trim (loss).

STEP 1. Identify the EPQ and the APQ.

APQ = 50 pounds (whole potatoes)
EPQ = 42.5 pounds (cleaned and peeled potatoes)

STEP 2. Determine if the units are the same before calculating the yield percent. Use the bridge method (Chapter 4, page 50) if necessary. In this problem, both the EPQ and the APQ are in pounds. We can continue.

STEP 3. Substitute the weights of the EPQ and APQ into the formula and solve.

$$\text{Yield percent} = \frac{\text{EPQ}}{\text{APQ}} = \frac{42.5 \text{ lb}}{50 \text{ lb}} = 0.85 \times 100 = 85\%$$

The calculations indicate that the yield percent for potatoes is 85 percent.

It is important to recognize that the 10 pounds of potatoes or the as-purchased quantity represents 100 percent. After fabricating the potatoes there will be a pile of peeled potatoes and a pile of peels (trim). The 8.5 pounds of cleaned potatoes (the edible portion quantity) represents 85 percent of the as-purchased quantity; this is the yield percent. The percent that is not usable in this application is the trim loss percent, in this case 15 percent (100% − 85% = 15%). The yield percent and the trim loss percent add up to 100 percent, and the EPQ and trim add up to the APQ. See the diagram at right.

ROUNDING

Yield percent is a mathematical prediction of the percent of a food that is usable. In this case, we are predicting that 45.6 percent of the lemons, by weight, will be juice when squeezed. We could leave that number as is (45.6 percent) or we could round it. Rules of mathematics say to round such a figure up; however, rounding it up to 46 percent would allot a greater yield to the lemons. As a rule, yield percent should be truncated at the whole percent, 45 percent, to ensure that enough product is ordered to provide the necessary yield.

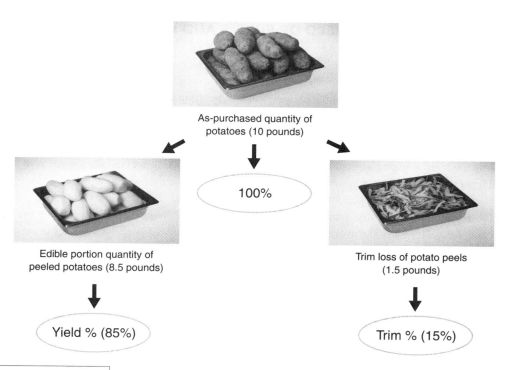

As-purchased quantity of
potatoes (10 pounds)

100%

Edible portion quantity of
peeled potatoes (8.5 pounds)

Trim loss of potato peels
(1.5 pounds)

Yield % (85%)

Trim % (15%)

EXAMPLE 2:

You purchase a 5-pound bag of lemons and juice them. When you finish, you have 36.5 ounces of lemon juice. What is the yield percent for lemon juice?

STEP 1. Identify the EPQ and the APQ.

APQ = 5 pounds (whole lemons)
EPQ = 36.5 ounces (lemon juice)

STEP 2. Determine if the units are the same before calculating the yield percent. Use the bridge method (Chapter 4, page 50) if necessary. In this case, the units are not the same. Let's convert the 36.5 ounces to pounds.

$$\frac{36.5 \ \cancel{oz}}{1} \times \frac{1 \ lb}{16 \ \cancel{oz}} = \frac{36.5}{16} = 2.28125 \ lb \ of \ lemon \ juice$$

Now that both values are in pounds, proceed. Keep in mind that the APQ could have been converted so that both values were in ounces. Either approach would have the same end result.

STEP 3. Substitute the EPQ and APQ values into the formula and solve.

$$Yield \ percent = \frac{EPQ}{APQ} = \frac{2.28125 \ lb}{5 \ lb} = 0.456 \times 100 = 45.6\%$$

After rounding, it is safe to say that 45 percent of the weight of the lemons purchased will be juice.

93

THE APPROXIMATE YIELD OF FRUITS AND VEGETABLES CHART

Yield percent is a necessary tool. The following chart is designed to provide yield information for a sampling of fruits and vegetables. Keep in mind that the yield percent for the listed fruits and vegetables may vary depending on how you will be using them. Different ways of fabricating fruits or vegetables will result in different yield percents. For instance, the yield percent for cantaloupe is different when you are preparing melon balls than when you are cutting the melon into slices or chunks. The problems that appear in this textbook use the information from the yield percent chart contained in this chapter. There are more extensive sources available, or you can perform your own yield tests to gather the information you require.

The chart provides the yield percents of the listed fruits and vegetables and information regarding the as-purchased weight of certain fruits and vegetables. For example, the listing for celery gives the average weight of a bunch of celery (2 pounds). Another example is coconut—the average weight of a coconut is 26 ounces. This information will become very useful in later chapters.

FACTORS THAT AFFECT YIELD PERCENT

The Approximate Yield of Fruits and Vegetables Chart gives approximate yield percents for a variety of fruits and vegetables. However, certain conditions may affect the yield percent:

- An employee's skill in cleaning the product will have an enormous effect on the yield percent. Some employees will clean a product using a heavy hand, resulting in more trim, whereas other employees will not create as much waste when cleaning the same product.

- The size of the product will also have an effect on the yield percent. Cleaning small carrots will create more waste and a lower yield percent than larger carrots cleaned in the same way because there is more surface area per unit of weight for the smaller carrots.

- The condition of the fruit or vegetable will have an effect on the yield percent. If the product is not used while it is fresh and in its best condition, the yield percent will be lower.

The Approximate Yield of Fruits and Vegetables Chart gives the yields for fruits and vegetables in their best condition with a highly skilled individual fabricating them. Remember, these yields are approximate; if an exact yield percent is needed for a particular situation, an actual yield test should be done. To do this, clean a sample of the product and calculate the exact yield percent using the following steps. Carrots are used in this example, but the same procedure should be followed for all fruits and vegetables.

STEPS FOR A YIELD TEST

STEP 1. Purchase carrots.

STEP 2. Weigh the carrots (APQ).

APPROXIMATE YIELD OF FRUITS AND VEGETABLES CHART

Approx. Wgt ea	Item	Yield %	Approx. Wgt ea	Item	Yield %
2 lb ea	Anise	75		Melons:	
	Apples	76		Cantaloupe	50
	Apricots	94		Casaba	50
	Artichokes	48		Crenshaw melon	50
	Asparagus	56		Honeydew, no rind	60
	Avocado	75		Watermelon, flesh	46
0.44 lb ea	Bananas	68		Mushrooms	97
	Beans, green or wax	88		Mustard greens	68
	Beans, lima, in shell	40		Nectarines	86
	Beet greens	56		Okra	78
	Beets, no tops	76	0.33 lb bunch	Onions, green (10–12)	60
	Beets, with tops	49		Onions, large	89
	Blackberries	92		Orange sections	70
	Blueberries	92	0.33 lb bunch	Parsley	76
1.5 lb bunch	Broccoli	61		Parsnips	85
	Brussels sprouts	74		Peaches	76
2.5 lb ea	Cabbage, green	79		Pears	78
	Cantaloupe, no rind	50		Peas, green, in the shell	38
	Carrots, no tops	82	0.19 lb ea	Peppers, fryers	85
	Carrots, with tops	60	0.33 lb ea	Peppers, green	82
2 lb head	Cauliflower	45		Persimmons	82
2 lb bunch	Celery	75	4 lb ea	Pineapple	52
	Celery root (celeriac)	75		Plums, pitted	85
	Chard	77		Pomegranates	54
26 oz ea	Coconut	53		Potatoes, chef	85
	Collards	77		Potatoes, red	81
0.58 lb ea	Cucumbers	95		Potatoes, sweet	80
1.25 lb ea	Eggplant	81		Radishes, no tops	85
	Endive, chicory, escarole	74		Radishes, with tops	63
	Figs	82		Raspberries	97
	Fruit for juice:			Rhubarb, no leaves	86
16 oz	Grapefruit	45*	3 lb ea	Rutabagas	85
3.5 oz	Lemon	45*		Salsify	63
2.2 oz	Lime	35*	0.03 lb ea	Shallots	89
6.6 oz	Orange, Fla.	50*		Spinach	74
0.125 lb ea	Garlic bulb (10–12 cloves)	87		Squash:	
	Grapefruit sections	47	0.83 lb ea	Acorn	78
	Grapes, seedless	94	1.8 lb ea	Butternut	52
	Kale	74		Hubbard	66
	Kohlrabi	55	0.36 lb ea	Yellow	95
0.75 lb bunch	Leeks	52	0.58 lb ea	Zucchini	95
2.25 lb head	Lettuce, iceberg	74		Strawberries	87
	Lettuce, leaf	67			

*The yield percent of producing juice.

95

STEP 3. Clean the carrots (peel them and trim the ends).

STEP 4. Weigh the clean carrots (EPQ).

STEP 5. Using the APQ and EPQ weights, calculate the yield percent using the formula discussed in the beginning of the chapter.

BUTCHER'S YIELD TEST

The butcher's yield test is very similar to the yield test for fruits and vegetables just explained. The main difference is that the trim created during the fabrication of meat and poultry has value, whereas the trim created when you fabricate fruits and vegetables generally does not. There are several definitions and calculations for the butcher's yield test that are slightly different:

AS-PURCHASED WEIGHT: For meat and poultry, the APQ is the weight of the meat or poultry item as it is delivered from the purveyor.

TRIM: The trim of meat and poultry has three components:

> **FAT:** The weight of the fat removed during fabrication

> **BONES:** The weight of the bones removed during fabrication

> **USABLE TRIM:** The weight of the trim that can be used in other preparations (ground beef, cubed beef for stew, chicken wings, etc.)

NEW FABRICATED WEIGHT: The new fabricated weight is the as-purchased weight minus the total trim weight.

$$\text{Butcher's yield percent} = \frac{\text{New fabricated weight}}{\text{As-purchased weight}} \times 100$$

EXAMPLE:

You purchase rib meat that weighs 36.9 pounds. The fat weighs 8 pounds, the bones weigh 7.3 pounds, and the usable trim weighs 8.7 pounds. To calculate the butcher's yield percent, you must first follow the steps to calculate the new fabricated weight.

STEP 1. Add up the weight of the trim.

$$8 \text{ pounds} + 7.3 \text{ pounds} + 8.7 \text{ pounds} = 24 \text{ pounds}$$

STEP 2. Subtract the trim weight from the as-purchased weight to find the new fabricated weight.

$$36.9 \text{ pounds} - 24 \text{ pounds} = 12.9 \text{ pounds}$$

STEP 3. To find the butcher's yield, substitute the as-purchased weight and the new fabricated weight.

$$\text{Butcher's yield percent} = \frac{\text{New fabricated weight}}{\text{As-purchased weight}} \times 100$$

$$= \frac{12.9 \cancel{\text{ lb}}}{36.9 \cancel{\text{ lb}}} \times 100 = 0.349 \times 100 = 34.9\%, \text{ or } 34\%$$

CHAPTER REVIEW

The concept of yield percent is very important when determining how much of a product to purchase or use for a recipe. It would be awful to place an order for a quantity of product listed in the recipe and then discover that you are short because the yield percent was not taken into account! Many chefs guess at the EPQ and APQ of ingredients that they are using. Sometimes they are right; sometimes they are wrong. Now you have the tools to be correct all the time. The only thing to remember is that you must monitor the fabrication skills of the people trimming the products you are using.

DEFINITIONS TO REMEMBER

AS-PURCHASED QUANTITY (APQ) is defined as the weight, volume, or count of the nonfabricated fruit or vegetable. In other words, it is the quantity (weight, volume, or count) of the product as it is received from the vendor.

EDIBLE PORTION QUANTITY (EPQ) is defined as the weight, volume, or count of the fabricated fruit or vegetable. In other words, it is the quantity (weight, volume, or count) of the product after it has been cleaned, peeled, or prepared (fabricated) and is ready for use.

TRIM is defined as the weight or volume of the waste. Trim, mathematically speaking, is the difference between APQ and EPQ:

$$\text{APQ} - \text{EPQ} = \text{Trim}$$

YIELD PERCENT FORMULA:

$$\text{Yield percent} = \frac{\text{EPQ}}{\text{APQ}} \times 100$$

EPQ, APQ, and Yield Percent Triangle

97

CHAPTER PRACTICE

Answers to odd-numbered questions may be found on page 251.

Leave your answers in decimal form. Final answers should be truncated at the ten-thousandths place value (for example, 10.456789 should be left as 10.4567). Percent answers should be truncated at the whole percent (for example, 78.6% becomes 78%).

1. Name 3 fruits and vegetables with a very low yield percent.

_____

_____

_____

_____

_____

2. Name 3 fruits and vegetables with a very high yield percent.

_____

_____

_____

_____

3. Chef Linda bought 4 bunches of basil for a recipe for a brunch she is catering. Each bunch weighs 2.5 ounces, and 5.6 ounces of usable basil are yielded from all the cleaned bunches. What is the yield percent?

_____

_____

_____

_____

4. You purchased 25 pounds of sweet potatoes. After cleaning the potatoes, there are 6.25 pounds of peels. What is the yield percent?

_____

_____

_____

_____

5. You purchase 6 heads of Bibb lettuce. Each head weighs 6 ounces. After cleaning the lettuce, you have 1.8 pounds of trimmed lettuce. What is the yield percent?

_____

_____

_____

_____

_____

6. You purchase 25 bananas. Each banana weighs approximately 0.44 pounds. After peeling and trimming the fruit, you have 7.1875 pounds of cleaned bananas. What is the yield percent?

_____

_____

_____

_____

_____

7. You purchase a case of beets that weighs 40 pounds. After cleaning the beets, you have 13 pounds 9.6 ounces of trim. What is the yield percent?

_____

_____

_____

_____

_____

8. Chef Julia is serving Green Bean Salad with Feta Cheese, Tomatoes, and Olives. She is serving 5-ounce portions to each of the 175 guests. She will need 43.75 pounds of cleaned green beans. She orders 50 pounds of green beans. What is the yield percent?

_____

_____

_____

_____

_____

9. You have 10 pounds of anise. After cleaning it, you have 7 pounds 8 ounces of trimmed anise. You are serving 25 people. What is the yield percent?

_____

_____

_____

_____

_____

10. You have 25 pounds of leaf lettuce. After cleaning the lettuce, you have 8 pounds 4 ounces of outer leaves and cores. What is the yield percent?

_____

_____

_____

_____

_____

11. The trim loss percent for kohlrabi is 45 percent. What is the yield percent?

_____

_____

_____

_____

_____

12. You purchase 10.375 pounds of apples in order to have enough apples to make 4 pies. Each pie is to contain 2 pounds 1 ounce of cleaned apples. What is the yield percent for the apples?

_____

_____

_____

_____

_____

13. You have 6 cabbages, each weighing 2.25 pounds. If after cleaning the cabbages you are left with 170 ounces of usable cabbage, what is the yield percent?

_____

_____

_____

_____

_____

14. You have 9 red peppers, each weighing $5\frac{1}{3}$ ounces. The trim weighs 17 percent of the purchased amount, and the edible portion quantity is $2\frac{1}{2}$ pounds. What is the yield percent?

_____

_____

_____

_____

_____

15. Explain which fruit would have a higher yield percent when used to make fruit salad, strawberries, or cantaloupe.

_____

_____

_____

_____

_____

16. Define yield percent in your own words. How would a chef use yield percent?

_____

_____

_____

_____

_____

17. You purchase a basket of mushrooms, which weighs 1 kilogram. After cleaning the mushrooms you have 33 ounces remaining. What is the yield percent for the mushrooms?

_____

_____

_____

_____

_____

18. You purchase 28 bunches of cauliflower. Each bunch of cauliflower weighs 2 pounds. After cleaning and trimming the cauliflower you are left with 25 pounds 3 ounces of clean cauliflower. What is the yield percent for the cauliflower?

_____

_____

_____

_____

_____

19. You determine the trim loss percent for kiwi is 15 percent. What is the yield percent?

_____

_____

_____

_____

20. If you calculate a yield percent for an ingredient to be 82.8 percent, why is it better to use 82 percent and not 83 percent in your calculation?

_____

_____

_____

_____

_____

21. The following yield percents are incorrect. Explain why they do not make sense and, without looking them up, estimate a more appropriate yield percent for each.

    A. Peaches, peeled and pitted   131%

_____

_____

_____

_____

    B. Mushrooms, cleaned and sliced   7%

_____

_____

_____

_____

C. Cantaloupe, peeled and seeded   92.6%

_____
_____
_____
_____
_____

22. You purchase 10 pounds of cucumbers. Each cucumber weighs approximately 10 ounces.

    A. How many cucumbers would you expect to receive in the 10-pound order?

_____
_____
_____
_____
_____

    B. You peel and seed 2 cucumbers and have 9 ounces of peels and seeds. What is the yield percent?

_____
_____
_____
_____
_____

23. The loss percent for Jerusalem artichokes is 32 percent. What is the yield percent?

_____
_____
_____
_____
_____

24. The yield percent on horse (jumbo) carrots is 85 percent. The yield percent for regular carrots is 82 percent. Explain why there is a difference in the yield percents.

_____
_____
_____
_____
_____

25. You purchase a crate of pumpkins that weighs 50#. After cleaning and seeding the pumpkins you have 31 pounds 8 ounces of clean pumpkin. What is the yield percent for the pumpkin?

_____

_____

_____

_____

_____

26. Four stalks of rhubarb weigh 1 pound. You purchase 30 stalks, and after trimming the rhubarb you have 6 pounds 14 ounces of clean rhubarb. What is the yield percent?

_____

_____

_____

_____

27. At a winery 15 people are hired to pick grapes. They pick 15 tons of grapes, which yield 1,200 to 1,300 gallons of wine (1 ton = 2,000 pounds). What is the yield percent for grapes to produce wine? (Use 1,250 gallons in calculations.)

_____

_____

_____

_____

28. You receive 5 bunches of collard greens. Each bunch weighs 12 ounces. After cleaning you have 2 pounds 7 ounces of cleaned collard greens. What is the yield percent for collard greens?

_____

_____

_____

_____

_____

29. You have $8\frac{1}{2}$ pounds of whole pistachios that you want to use for ice cream. You are left with $4\frac{1}{4}$ pounds after you shell the nuts. What is the yield percent for the pistachio nuts?

_____

_____

_____

_____

_____

30. You are making guacamole and have purchased 10 pounds of avocados. After cleaning you have 7 pounds 13 ounces of cleaned avocado left. What is the yield percent for the avocado?

_____

_____

_____

_____

_____

Applying Yield Percent

8

Y ou have been hired to cater a party for 150 people and will be making your famous apple pie. Your calculations show that you will need 52½ pounds of peeled, cored, and sliced apples to make the 15 pies necessary to serve 150 people. Would it be reasonable to order 52½ or even 53 pounds of apples? If you ordered that quantity of apples and then peeled, cored, and sliced them, the cleaned apples would weigh significantly less, and there would not be enough apples to make the pies.

It is important to remember that the trim loss—in this case, the peels and cores—must be taken into account when ordering any fresh fruit or vegetable. An accurate prediction of the amount of fruit needed would eliminate the possibility of over- or underordering.

In Chapter 7, page 87, the math of yield percent was introduced. This chapter investigates the application of yield percent to solve this situation and others like it.

OBJECTIVES

- Calculate the as-purchased quantity when the edible portion quantity is given.

- Calculate the edible portion quantity when the as-purchased quantity is given.

CALCULATING THE AS-PURCHASED QUANTITY

It is necessary to consider the trim loss when purchasing items, but many recipes list ingredients in edible portion amounts. If you confuse the as-purchased quantity with the edible portion quantity, the recipe may not work, or it may not yield the number of portions desired (see Chef's Note on page 88). For purchasing, the edible portion quantity must be converted to the as-purchased quantity.

Using the yield percent, this can be calculated.

$$\text{As-purchased quantity (APQ)} = \frac{\text{Edible portion quantity (EPQ)}}{\text{Yield percent (in decimal form)}}$$

EXAMPLE:

It has already been determined that $52\frac{1}{2}$ pounds of cleaned apples are needed to make the apple pies for the party discussed in the chapter introduction, and apples have a 76 percent yield. The formula above can be applied to this situation to calculate the amount of apples that should be ordered to make the 15 pies:

$$APQ = \frac{EPQ}{\text{Yield percent}} = \frac{52.5 \text{ lb}}{0.76} = 69.07 \text{ lb (APQ) or 70 lb}$$

The minimum amount of apples that should be ordered to be sure that there are enough apples for the pies is 70 pounds.

> **ROUNDING NOTE**
> When calculating amounts to order, always round up. If the amount were rounded down, the order quantity would be underestimated.

Yield percent takes into account only the trim loss that occurs during fabrication of the apples. Other losses may occur, such as:

- Theft

- Spoilage

- Excessive waste (the yield percent may not really be 76 percent) due to the poor skill level of the person fabricating the product or a lack of quality in the product

- Mistakes in the kitchen, including burning, dropping, or contamination

The APQ can be calculated precisely, but it is important to remember that human and other uncontrollable errors or conditions may occur in a commercial kitchen and need to be considered.

107

CALCULATING THE EDIBLE PORTION QUANTITY

ROUNDING NOTE
The number of portions should be rounded down, since it would not be feasible to serve a partial portion to a guest. (See Appendix D, page 248).

Sometimes it is necessary to determine how many portions can be created from the as-purchased quantity. The amount of cleaned product (edible portion quantity) that can be obtained from a purchased item can be determined using the formula below. Once the edible portion quantity has been calculated, the number of portions that can be obtained can also be calculated.

$$\text{Edible portion quantity (EPQ)} = \frac{\text{As-purchased}}{\text{quantity (APQ)}} \times \frac{\text{Yield percent}}{\text{(in decimal form)}}$$

EXAMPLE:

You purchased a case of fresh green beans that weighs 20 pounds. How many $\frac{1}{4}$-pound servings of cleaned green beans are in the case? First, you should look up the yield percent for green beans (see Chapter 7, page 91). You will find that the yield is 88 percent. Next, you can compute the weight of the beans after cleaning.

$$\text{Edible portion quantity} = \text{APQ} \times \text{Yield percent}$$

$$= 20 \text{ lb} \times 0.88 = 17.6 \text{ lb}$$

The calculation shows that the edible portion quantity would be 17.6 pounds. Now you can calculate how many $\frac{1}{4}$-pound portions of cleaned green beans can be served from 17.6 pounds of cleaned green beans.

$$\text{Number of servings} = \frac{\text{Edible portion quantity}}{\text{Portion size}}$$

$$= \frac{17.6 \text{ lb}}{0.25 \text{ lb}} = 70.4$$

You should be able to obtain 70 full servings from the case of green beans.

WHEN THE YIELD IS 100 PERCENT
It should be kept in mind that not all foods have a trim loss. Many foods have 100 percent yield, such as sugar, flour, or dried spices. Other foods have a yield percent that can change, depending on how they are served. For example, there is an important differenc between the yield percent for melon balls versus melon cubes.

THE EPQ, APQ, AND YIELD PERCENT TRIANGLE

This triangle was introduced in Chapter 7, page 91, as a tool to find the yield percent, as-purchased quantity, and edible portion quantity. It is mathematically identical to the part, whole, and percent triangle introduced in Chapter 1, page 12; the only difference is in the

Although a yield chart is helpful, a food-service professional must keep in mind how an item will be used in a dish. If only the florets of the broccoli are being used, the yield percent is much lower than if the stalks would also be used.

terms used. So do not think of this as another tool to learn; think of it as a variation of what you already know.

PART = Edible portion quantity

WHOLE = As-purchased quantity

PERCENT = Yield percent

STEPS FOR USING THE EPQ, APQ, AND YIELD PERCENT TRIANGLE

STEP 1. Determine what you are looking for: EPQ, APQ, or yield percent.

STEP 2. *To find the edible portion quantity (EPQ)*
Cover the EPQ for edible portion quantity.

APQ and % are side by side. This directs you to multiply the APQ by the yield percent. (Remember to change the percent to a decimal by dividing by 100.)

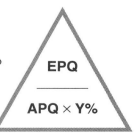

$$\frac{EPQ}{APQ \times Y\%}$$

To find the as-purchased quantity (APQ)

Cover the APQ for as-purchased quantity.

EPQ is over Y%. This directs you to divide the EPQ by the yield percent. (Remember to change the percent to a decimal by dividing by 100.)

To find the yield percent

Cover the Y% for yield percent.

EPQ is over APQ. This directs you to divide the EPQ by the APQ and multiply the answer by 100 to convert it to the yield percent.

CHAPTER REVIEW

Yield percent is a useful tool for a professional chef. Mastering this concept will allow you to approach purchasing decisions in a logical and organized manner. In addition, you will determine of the number of portions that can be prepared from a particular amount of product. Mastering these formulas will prevent you from making costly, time-consuming, and embarrassing errors.

The following formulas and the triangle (a study tool) are very important to remember:

Calculating the as-purchased quantity:

$$\text{As-purchased quantity (APQ)} = \frac{\text{Edible portion quantity (EPQ)}}{\text{Yield percent (in decimal form)}}$$

Calculating the edible portion quantity:

$$\text{Edible portion quantity (EPQ)} = \frac{\text{As-purchased}}{\text{quantity (APQ)}} \times \frac{\text{Yield percent}}{\text{(in decimal form)}}$$

CHAPTER PRACTICE

Answers to odd-numbered questions may be found on page 251.

Solve the following problems. If necessary, refer to the Approximate Yield of Fruits and Vegetables Chart on page 95. Round your answer to the most reasonable whole number or whole item at the end of your calculations.

1. You are serving 5 ounces of iceberg lettuce to each of the 95 guests at a party you are catering. How many heads of lettuce should you purchase?

_____

_____

_____

_____

_____

2. A recipe for baba ghannuj (puréed roasted eggplant) requires 1 $\frac{1}{2}$ ounces of puréed eggplant for each serving. If you make enough baba ghannuj to serve 300 people, how many eggplants should you purchase?

_____

_____

_____

_____

_____

3. You need two hundred fifty 2-ounce portions of fresh anise. How many anises should you purchase?

_____

_____

_____

_____

_____

4. You have a case of green cabbage. Each case contains 15 cabbages. If you want to provide servings of 2 $\frac{1}{2}$ ounces, how many servings can you expect to get out of the case?

_____

_____

_____

_____

_____

5. You have 7 zucchinis. How many zucchini cheddar breads can you make if each recipe calls for 1 cup of grated zucchini? Each cup of zucchini weighs 5 ounces, and 1 zucchini weighs 0.58 pounds.

_____

_____

_____

_____

_____

For Questions 6–13, calculate the as-purchased quantity (APQ). Note: Starred items (*) are usually purchased singly or by the bunch. See the Approximate Yield of Fruits and Vegetables Chart on page 95.

Recipe Item	Recipe Quantity	Yield %	As-Purchased Quantity
6. Bananas, sliced	5 lb 6 oz	_____	_____ bananas
7. Blackberries	2 kg	_____	_____ pounds
8. Broccoli, trimmed*	7½ lb	_____	_____ bunches
9. Nectarines	6 lb 12 oz	_____	_____ pounds
10. Celery, julienned*	1¾ lb	_____	_____ bunches
11. Plums, pitted	8 lb	_____	_____ pounds
12. Garlic, finely diced	175 g	_____	_____ ounces
13. Pineapples*	10 lb	_____	_____ pineapples

14. The chef has asked you to prepare one hundred 6-ounce portions of broccoli. If the yield for broccoli is 60 percent, how many bunches of broccoli do you need to purchase?

_____

_____

_____

_____

_____

15. You purchase a bushel of apples, which weighs 28 pounds. You want to make apple cake with these apples. Each cake calls for 1 quart of peeled, chopped apples. If 1 cup of chopped apples weighs 3⅓ ounces, then how many cakes can you make?

_____

_____

_____

_____

_____

16. One hundred eighty people are coming for lunch, and you are serving each a 4-ounce portion of potatoes. One bag of red potatoes weighs 52 pounds. After peeling and trimming, the potatoes weigh 47 pounds 7 ounces. How many pounds of clean red potatoes will be left after lunch is served?

_____

_____

_____

_____

_____

17. If you purchase 6 bunches of celery, each weighing 2 pounds, and the yield percent is 75 percent, how many 2-ounce servings can be made?

_____

_____

_____

_____

_____

18. How many 5-ounce portions of peeled chef's potatoes will you have if you ordered 4 bags at 50 pounds each?

_____

_____

_____

_____

_____

19. Keely is having a party for 200 people. She is serving green beans and has purchased 50 pounds. If the yield is 88 percent, what size portion, in ounces, will each guest receive?

_____

_____

_____

_____

20. You have 12 pounds 6 ounces of Brussels sprouts. How many 3-ounce servings can be made if the yield percent is 74 percent?

_____

_____

_____

_____

_____

21. You want to serve a 4-ounce portion of eggplant to each guest. Is it correct to predict that with 12 eggplants you will be able to serve 60 guests? If this is incorrect, explain why, and calculate the correct answer.

_____

_____

_____

_____

_____

22. Chef Ben has 30 pounds of cleaned chicken breasts for the chicken entrée for the night. How many pounds of chicken were purchased if the yield percent is 20 percent?

_____

_____

_____

_____

_____

23. For a banquet of 480 people you are to prep broccoli in portions of 2 ½ ounces. You obtain 30 pounds of cleaned broccoli. How much broccoli must you purchase to complete the prep for the banquet if the yield percent is 61 percent?

_____

_____

_____

_____

_____

24. For every 30 pounds of green beans you purchase, you end up with 26 pounds of cleaned green beans. What is the yield percent for green beans? How many pounds should you order if you need 50 pounds of cleaned green beans?

_____

_____

_____

_____

_____

25. You are making peach pie for 265 guests and will need to prepare 34 pies. Each pie will require 0.75 kilograms of peeled, sliced peaches. How many pounds of peaches should you order?

_____

_____

_____

_____

_____

26. A bunch of leeks weighs 12 ounces. How many bunches of leeks must you order if a recipe calls for 2.5 kilograms of cleaned leeks and the yield percent is 54 percent?

_____

_____

_____

_____

_____

27. You have a recipe for mango sorbet that serves 70. The recipe calls for 3 quarts of fresh diced mango. If 1 cup of diced mango weighs 5.8 ounces and mangos have a 68 percent yield, how many pounds of mango should you order?

_____

_____

_____

_____

_____

28. You have ordered a box of imported berries from France. The box weighs 1.5 kilograms. The berries have a 97 percent yield. After puréeing the berries, how many ¹/₂-ounce servings will you be able to make?

_____

_____

_____

_____

29. You are preparing a plum cobbler. The recipe calls for 4 pounds of pitted plums. The yield percent for plums is 90 percent. After multiplying the 4 pounds by the yield percent, you determine that you should order 3.6 pounds. If you order 4 pounds of plums, will you have enough? If not, correct the math error and determine the correct answer.

_____

_____

_____

_____

30. You need to calculate how many 3-ounce portions of green beans are in a 40-pound box of green beans. After you do the calculations, you determine you could serve 1,500 people. Explain why this is wrong and calculate the correct answer.

_____

_____

_____

_____

31. You are making apple pies. Each pie needs 2 pounds 9 ounces of cleaned apples. How many apple pies can be made from 20 pounds of apples if the yield is 82 percent?

_____

_____

_____

_____

32. You wish to serve 115 people a 4-ounce portion of fresh cubed pineapple each. How many pineapples must you purchase?

_____

_____

_____

_____

_____

33. You are making dinner for 13 guests. One of the recipes you are making calls for 3 cups of chopped onion. How many pounds of onions should you order?

_____

_____

_____

_____

_____

34. You purchase a case of cantaloupes containing 15 cantaloupes. Each cantaloupe weighs 3 pounds. You are making melon balls with all the cantaloupes and serving them in 3-ounce portions. The yield percent for cantaloupe when making melon balls is 38 percent. How many servings can be made from the case of cantaloupes?

_____

_____

_____

_____

_____

35. You are preparing mango salsa for 120 guests. Each plate will have 2 ounces of mango on it. Mangos are purchased by the piece. Each mango weighs 11 ounces before it is cleaned. The yield percent for mango is 69 percent. How many mangos should you purchase?

_____

_____

_____

_____

_____

36. You are serving 160 guests a ¹/₂-cup portion of cubed watermelon. Each watermelon weighs 20 pounds before it is cleaned. If 1 cup of cubed watermelon weighs 5 ounces, how many whole watermelons should you order?

_____

_____

_____

_____

_____

37. You have 6 pineapples, each weighing 4 pounds. The recipe for Pineapple Salsa calls for 6 pounds of clean pineapple. How many times can you make the salsa?

_____

_____

_____

_____

_____

38. You receive a case of Florida oranges containing 72 oranges. How many liters of juice will the case produce?

_____

_____

_____

_____

_____

39. You are making 25 plum tortes. Each plum weighs 3 ounces. The recipe calls for 18 ounces of pitted plums per torte. How many pounds of plums should you order?

_____

_____

_____

_____

_____

40. You are making strawberry pie. The recipe calls for 1 ½ pints of cleaned, sliced strawberries. If the yield percent for strawberries is 91 percent and 1 cup of clean, sliced strawberries weighs 7 ounces, how many pounds of strawberries should you order?

_____

_____

_____

_____

_____

Finding Cost

You are catering a wedding brunch for 230 guests. You predict that each guest will have 2 pieces of a special prosciutto appetizer that you are preparing. A pound of prosciutto will make 48 appetizers. The bride has requested an imported prosciutto from Italy. This prosciutto can be purchased for $30 a kilogram. You need to estimate the cost of the prosciutto for this brunch in order to determine how much to charge.

One of the most important parts in budgeting and predicting is finding the cost of producing recipes. Most food items purchased from suppliers are packed and priced using wholesale bulk sizes, such as crates, cases, bags, and cartons. In kitchen production, the quantity in the package may be used for several different menu items. In order to allocate the proper prices to the recipe being prepared, it is necessary to convert the price of the purchase package into unit prices, which are expressed by the price per pound, each, dozen, quart, and so on, depending on how the product is used in the recipe.

Another example might be that you have just received a case of canned Italian plum tomatoes that you ordered for the lasagna you are making. The purchase price is $18.78, and there are six cans in a case. From this information, you can find the price per can (per item). With the two values (price per can and the amount needed for the recipe), the cost for plum tomatoes in the recipe can be calculated.

Finding cost is an integral part of a successful food-service operation.

It is very important to realize that no matter how good the food is, the ability to calculate food cost as a tool in controlling cost directly relates to success.

DETERMINING COST PER UNIT

The price paid for goods is the as-purchased cost. Products are purchased in many units, such as cases, pounds, bushels, containers, ounces, grams, kilograms, liters, gallons, and dozens. Products may also be used in recipes in these same units. However, occasionally a product is purchased in a unit that differs from the unit used in the recipe. For instance, a recipe calls for 10 ounces of flour, but flour is purchased in 50-pound bags. It will be necessary to determine the cost per unit to determine the cost of an ingredient in this or any other recipe or dish.

To find the cost of one unit in a pack with many units, always divide the as-purchased cost (total cost) of the pack by the number of units in the pack.

$$\text{Cost per unit} = \frac{\text{As-purchased cost}}{\text{Number of units}}$$

The word *per* in this formula indicates that the cost for one unit is being calculated. The unit could be one of many things: 1 peach, 1 ounce, 1 pound, 1 package, or 1 can. When using the formula, remember that the amount of money always goes on top and the number of units goes on the bottom of the formula.

This formula is often used in everyday life. It is used while shopping in the supermarket to find the best price on almost any item. For example, the cost per unit of two brands of rice can be compared to see which is lower. If Brand A can be purchased in 1-pound boxes for $1.89 but Brand B can be purchased in a 5-pound bag for $4.96, which is cheaper? To compare these two items, the prices must be for the same unit. In other words, in this example, you need to find the price for 1 pound of rice in each package. This is the calculation that would have to be done to make the comparison:

$$\text{Cost per unit} = \frac{\text{As-purchased cost}}{\text{Number of units}} = \frac{\$4.96}{5 \text{ lb}}$$

$$= \$0.992 \text{ per lb}$$

121

This calculation indicates that 1 pound of Brand B would cost $1.00. That is less than the $1.89 for 1 pound of Brand A rice. Although the total cost of the rice is $4.96, the price per pound is less.

ROUNDING

In calculating cost it is important to pay attention to rounding techniques. For $0.992, the usual rounding rules would have you round down to $0.99. However, in costing, it is always better to round any partial cent up to the next higher cent to account for any partial pennies. If you rounded this amount down, you would be underestimating your cost by $0.01. This amount may not seem like a lot, but over hundreds of pounds these small differences could add up. So $0.992 would round to $1.00.

TOTAL COST

When calculating total cost in the food-service industry, it is important to remember that cost is based on how much of a product is used for a particular recipe, not on the total amount purchased. The as-purchased information is used to determine the cost per unit of the amount that is used in a particular recipe. If you are using 4 pounds of flour to make a wedding cake, but the flour is purchased in a 25-pound bag, you would want to allocate only the cost of 4 pounds of flour to the wedding cake, not the cost of 25 pounds. The cost of the remaining flour will be allocated to the other products made with the remaining 21 pounds.

ROUNDING NOTE

When calculating total cost, it is best not to round the number of units and the cost per unit. Rounding to the next higher cent should take place after the calculations are finished and the value for the total cost has been determined. Rounding in each step of the calculation may cause the answer to be significantly higher.

CALCULATING TOTAL COST

After the cost per unit has been calculated, the total cost formula may have to be applied to determine how much an ingredient in a particular recipe is costing you.

Total cost may be calculated using the following formula:

Total Cost = Number of units × Cost per unit

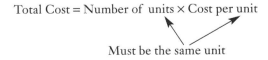

Must be the same unit

STEPS FOR CALCULATING TOTAL COST

STEP 1. Read the problem to determine the quantity you are costing.

STEP 2. Identify the given as-purchased cost information.

STEP 3. Select the unit to be used for both the as-purchased cost and the quantity.

STEP 4. Perform the calculations necessary to convert the cost per unit and/or the quantity to the unit chosen in step 3.

STEP 5. Substitute these numbers into the total cost formula and multiply to find the total cost.

STEP 6. Round any partial pennies up to the next highest cent.

STEP 7. Check the answer to make sure it is reasonable.

EXAMPLE 1:

You are catering a wedding brunch for 230 guests. You predict that each guest will have approximately 2 pieces of a special prosciutto appetizer that you are preparing. A pound of prosciutto will make 48 appetizers. The bride has requested an imported prosciutto from Italy. This prosciutto can be purchased for $30 a kilogram.

STEP 1. Read the problem and determine the quantity you are costing.

> We are costing 2 pieces of a special prosciutto appetizer for 230 guests.
>
> 230 × 2 appetizers = 460 appetizers total

STEP 2. Identify the given as-purchased cost information.

> The prosciutto costs $30 per kilogram.

STEP 3. Select the unit to be used for both the as-purchased cost and the quantity.

> Prosciutto is purchased by the kilogram, and 1 pound of prosciutto makes 48 appetizers. For this example, we will choose pounds as the unit, but it is not incorrect to use kilograms.

STEP 4. Perform the calculations necessary to convert the cost per unit and/or the quantity to the unit chosen in step 3.

> The prosciutto price is already given per kilogram, so it is only necessary to convert the price to the price per pound. To find the cost per unit:
>
> 1 kg = 2.21 lb (see Chapter 3, page 40, for metric conversion)

$$\frac{\$30}{2.21 \text{ lb}} = \$13.5746 \text{ per lb}$$

The quantity: $\frac{460 \text{ pieces}}{1} \times \frac{1 \text{ lb}}{48 \text{ pieces}} = 9.5833 \text{ lb}$

STEP 5. Substitute these numbers into the total cost formula and multiply to find the total cost.

$$\text{Total cost} = \text{Number of units} \times \text{Cost per unit}$$
$$= 9.5833 \text{ per lb} \times \$13.5746 \text{ per lb} = \$130.0894$$

STEP 6. Round any partial pennies up to the next highest cent.

The total cost is $130.09.

STEP 7. Check the answer to make sure it is reasonable.

EXAMPLE 2:

A recipe calls for 1 ½ teaspoons of dried tarragon leaves. One tablespoon of tarragon weighs 0.08 ounce. Tarragon is purchased in 4-ounce jars. Each jar costs $5.77. How much will the tarragon cost for this recipe?

STEP 1. Read the problem and determine the quantity you are costing.

We need to find the cost of 1 ½ teaspoons of tarragon.

STEP 2. Identify the given as-purchased cost information.

Tarragon is sold by the jar for $5.77.

STEP 3. Select the unit to be used for both the cost per unit and the quantity.

Since both the conversion and the cost are in ounces, it would make sense to choose ounces as the unit with which to solve this problem.

STEP 4. Perform the calculations necessary to convert the cost per unit and/or the quantity to the unit chosen in step 3.

Quantity: We can use the bridge method to convert the 1 ½ teaspoons of tarragon to ounces, as described in Chapter 4.

$$\frac{1.5 \text{ tsp}}{1} \times \frac{1 \text{ tbsp}}{3 \text{ tsp}} = \frac{1.5}{3} = 0.5 \text{ tbsp}$$

$$\frac{0.5 \text{ \sout{tbsp}}}{1} \times \frac{0.08 \text{ oz}}{1 \text{ \sout{tbsp}}} = 0.04 \text{ oz}$$

Cost per Unit: To find the cost per ounce for tarragon, we will use the cost per unit formula:

$$\text{Cost per unit} = \frac{\text{As-purchased cost}}{\text{Number of units}} = \frac{\$5.77}{4 \text{ oz}} = \$1.4425 \text{ per oz}$$

STEP 5. Substitute these numbers into the total cost formula and multiply to find the total cost.

$$\text{Total cost} = \text{Number of units} \times \text{Cost per unit}$$
$$= 0.04 \text{ oz} \times \$1.4425 \text{ per oz} = \$0.0577$$

STEP 6. Round any partial pennies up to the next highest cent.

The amount $0.0577 rounds up to $0.06.

STEP 7. Check the answer to make sure it is reasonable.

When solving for total cost, any related unit may be selected to use in the equation. For the last problem, jars, teaspoons, tablespoons, ounces, or pounds could have been chosen. It usually requires fewer calculations to convert to a weight value (ounces or pounds). In addition, knowing the cost per ounce or pound of a given ingredient is more useful because it has many applications. Sometimes volume measure may be selected for the calculations if the product is bought and used in a volume quantity.

CHAPTER REVIEW

Finding the cost per unit and total cost for ingredients you will be using in the kitchen is necessary for recipe costing, which will be covered in Chapter 11. If you do not take the time to determine these amounts, you will be unable to properly estimate your cost for menu items produced in your kitchen. As a result, you will also be unable to find a selling price that will offer you a reasonable profit.

DETERMINING COST PER UNIT

$$\text{Cost per unit} = \frac{\text{As-purchased cost}}{\text{Number of units}}$$

CALCULATING TOTAL COST

Total cost may be calculated using the following formula:

$$\text{Total Cost} = \text{Number of units} \times \text{Cost per unit}$$

Must be the same unit

STEPS FOR CALCULATING TOTAL COST

STEP 1. Read the problem to determine the quantity you are costing.

STEP 2. Identify the given as-purchased cost information.

STEP 3. Select the unit to be used for both the as-purchased cost and the quantity.

STEP 4. Perform the calculations necessary to convert the cost per unit and/or the quantity to the unit chosen in step 3.

STEP 5. Substitute these numbers into the total cost formula and multiply to find the total cost.

STEP 6. Round any partial pennies up to the next highest cent.

STEP 7. Check the answer to make sure it is reasonable.

CHAPTER PRACTICE

Answers to odd-numbered questions may be found on page 251.

Round your final answers up to the next whole cent at the completion of your calculations.

1. Find the cost per fluid ounce and cost per can for a six-pack of soda (six 12-fl-oz cans) that sells for $1.99.

_____

_____

_____

_____

_____

2. Find the cost per ounce, cost per pound, and cost per head for a case of lettuce that costs $25 and contains 24 heads that weigh 26 ounces each.

_____

_____

_____

_____

_____

3. You purchase 5 pounds of smoked sharp cheddar cheese for $28. How much would 1 quart of grated smoked sharp cheddar cheese cost?

_____

_____

_____

_____

_____

4. Find the cost per fluid ounce and the cost per bottle for olive oil that comes in a case of six 1-gallon bottles and sells for $73.50 per case.

_____

_____

_____

_____

_____

Find the cost per unit of the following items.

Item	Pack	As-Purchased Cost	Cost per Unit
5. Asparagus	30 lb/crate	$93.90	_____/lb
6. Celery	30 bunch/crate	$19.50	_____/bunch
7. Cucumber	48 lb (60 ea)/bushel	$13.92	_____/ea
8. Escarole	18 lb (12 ea)/crate	$15.72	_____/ea
9. Lettuce	24 heads/crate	$17.00	_____/head
10. Parsley	60 bunch/bushel	$12.60	_____/bunch
11. Potatoes	50 lb	$13.50	_____/lb
12. Tomatoes, cherry	12 pt/case	$16.96	_____/pt

127

13. A 12-pound box of steaks is ordered. The steak costs $6.99 per pound. If each steak weighs 6 ounces, what is the cost per steak, and how many steaks are in each box?

_____

_____

_____

_____

_____

14. You want to serve 210 people each a 6-fluid-ounce portion of orange juice. Orange juice concentrate is purchased by the case for $22.80. Each case contains 12 cans, and each can makes $3/4$ gallon. How much will the juice cost for the 210 people?

_____

_____

_____

_____

_____

Use the given information to answer the following questions:

15. You purchase a case of Peck's Special Super Hot Mustard directly from the manufacturer for $71.82. Each case contains 18 jars, and each jar contains 8 ounces of mustard. One tablespoon of mustard weighs 18 grams.

A. What would one jar of mustard cost?

_____

_____

_____

_____

_____

B. What would 1 ounce of mustard cost?

_____

_____

_____

_____

_____

C. What would 1 teaspoon of mustard cost?

_____

_____

_____

_____

_____

D. How much would ¾ cup of mustard cost?

_____

_____

_____

_____

_____

16. Elizabeth's Cranberry Chutney is available by the case for $59.88. Each case contains 12 jars. Each 10-fluid-ounce jar contains 12 ounces of chutney. A tablespoon of chutney weighs 0.6 ounce.

A. How much will 1 tablespoon of chutney cost?

_____

_____

_____

_____

_____

B. What is the cost per ounce of chutney?

_____

_____

_____

_____

_____

C. If you need 2 cups of chutney to make a special salad, how much will the 2 cups cost?

_____

_____

_____

_____

_____

D. How much would a pound of chutney cost?

_____

_____

_____

_____

_____

17. Cumin can be purchased in 12-ounce containers for $7.95. It can also be purchased in a 3-ounce container for $3.99. Which is the better price?

_____

_____

_____

_____

_____

18. How much would 1 ¾ cups of milk cost if you purchase milk by the gallon for $2.39?

_____

_____

_____

_____

_____

19. If a 3.5-ounce portion of frozen spinach costs $0.25, how much would a 5-pound box cost?

_____

_____

_____

_____

_____

20. Bob bought 22 chickens. Each chicken weighs 3.5 pounds. The chickens cost Bob $81.62. How much did each chicken cost, and what is the cost per pound?

_____

_____

_____

_____

_____

21. A can of imported tuna weighs 2 kilograms and costs $15.98. White tuna costs $3.11 for a 13-ounce can. Which is the better buy?

_____

_____

_____

_____

_____

22. You purchase a case of dried cherries for $52.00. The case contains fourteen 12-ounce packages. What is the cost per pound? What is the cost per ounce?

_____

_____

_____

_____

_____

23. A case of cornmeal is priced at $12.96. Each case holds 12 containers of cornmeal. If there is 1 pound 8 ounces of cornmeal in each container, how much would 1 pound of cornmeal cost?

_____

_____

_____

_____

_____

24. You make 12 cakes for a total cost of $71.52. Each cake is to be cut into 12 portions. How much does each cake cost you to make? How much does one slice of cake cost?

_____

_____

_____

_____

_____

25. You are serving pineapple juice to a party of 170 people. Each person will receive a 6-ounce portion. You purchase pineapple juice by the half gallon for $1.69. How much will the 170 portions cost?

_____

_____

_____

_____

_____

26. You purchase currant jelly for $22.20 per case. Each case contains 4 jars, and each jar contains 4 pounds of jelly. How much would a pound of jelly cost? How much would one half cup of jelly cost?

_____

_____

_____

_____

_____

27. If you purchase 3 gallons of milk for $5.97, how much would 1 quart cost? How much would 1 fluid ounce cost? How much would 1 cup cost?

_____

_____

_____

_____

_____

28. A box of shrimp (26 to 30 per lb) costs $34.95. Each box contains 5 pounds of shrimp. What is the cost per shrimp? (Use the lowest count to solve the problem.) What is the cost per pound of shrimp?

_____

_____

_____

_____

_____

29. 180 grams of goat cheese costs $3.50. How much would 1 pound cost?

_____

_____

_____

_____

_____

30. A recipe calls for 3 cups of cornstarch. One cup of cornstarch weighs 4.5 ounces. How much would 1 cup cost if the price of cornstarch was $0.89 per pound?

_____

_____

_____

_____

31. You are baking 48 loaves of cranberry bread. It takes $\frac{1}{2}$ cup of dried cranberries to make one loaf of cranberry bread. If cranberries cost $1.75 per pound and 1 cup of cranberries weighs 6 ounces, what will the cranberries cost for the 48 loaves of bread?

_____

_____

_____

_____

_____

32. How much would 1 teaspoon of cumin cost if 1 cup of cumin weighs 4 ounces and 1 pound of cumin costs $10.60?

_____

_____

_____

_____

_____

133

33. You are hosting a party for 25 people. A recipe for walnut bread serves 5 people and calls for ⅓ cup of walnuts. If 1 cup of walnuts weighs 4 ounces and walnuts are purchased for $3.50 a pound, how much will the walnuts cost for the party?

_____

_____

_____

_____

_____

34. A recipe calls for ¼ cup of chili powder. Chili powder is purchased in an 18-ounce container for $9.95. How much would the ¼ cup of chili powder cost if 1 tablespoon of chili powder weighs 0.25 ounce?

_____

_____

_____

_____

_____

35. How much would 1 ¾ cups of cocoa powder cost if cocoa powder is purchased in 50-pound bags for $45.57 and 1 tablespoon of cocoa powder weighs 0.25 ounce?

_____

_____

_____

_____

_____

36. A 5-kilogram bag of cake flour costs $4.18. You are baking a cake that requires 3 ½ cups of cake flour. What will the flour cost to make this cake?

_____

_____

_____

_____

_____

37. You purchase 4 kilograms of Monterey jack cheese for $32.98. How much would 1 ounce cost? How much would 1 ½ cups of grated Monterey jack cheese cost?

_____

_____

_____

_____

_____

38. A recipe for pumpkin pie calls for 12 ounces of canned pumpkin. If you purchase pumpkin for $0.99 a can and each can contains 1 pound 2 ounces, then how much would the pumpkin for the pie cost?

_____

_____

_____

_____

_____

39. A 5.5-ounce jar of basil costs $3.41. How much would 5 grams cost?

_____

_____

_____

_____

_____

40. You purchase a 50-pound bag of pastry flour for $19.50. If 1 cup of pastry flour weighs 3 ⅓ ounces, then how much would 500 grams of pastry flour cost?

_____

_____

_____

_____

_____

41. For a party of 155 guests you are serving Black Bean Quesadillas. Each guest will have one quesadilla. One quesadilla requires a half cup of black beans. Black beans are purchased in cans and weigh 13.5 ounces when drained. One cup of drained beans weighs 6⅓ ounces. If you purchase beans by the case (12 cans per case) for $5.88, then how many cases of beans would you need to order and how much will the beans cost for the party? (Keep in mind that cost is based on what you use.)

_____

_____

_____

_____

_____

42. A jar of dill costs $7.64. If the jar contains 4 ounces of dill and 1 cup of dill weighs 2 ounces, then how much will 1 tablespoon cost?

_____

_____

_____

_____

_____

43. You purchase dried cherries in 8-ounce packages for $2.25. How much would 75 grams of dried cherries cost?

_____

_____

_____

_____

_____

44. A liter of extra-virgin olive oil costs $12.95. How much would 2 tablespoons cost?

_____

_____

_____

_____

_____

45. Chocolate fudge topping is purchased in 5-pound containers for $24. If 1 cup of chocolate fudge topping weighs 12 ounces, how much would ⅓ cup cost?

_____

_____

_____

_____

_____

Edible Portion Cost

Y ou are catering an autumn wedding for 240 guests. You will be serving Broccoli Rabe with Garlic and Hot Crushed Pepper to accompany Four-Cheese Lasagna. Sixty pounds of washed and trimmed broccoli rabe is needed to make this dish for this wedding; therefore, you should order a greater amount. If you just order the 60 pounds of broccoli rabe and then wash and trim it, you will not have enough to serve the 240 guests. You must order a greater amount of broccoli rabe to accommodate the waste from the trim.

This problem demonstrates the need to purchase more than the amount of cleaned fresh fruit or vegetables listed in the recipe in order to compensate for the fact that it will be trimmed. The concept of yield percent is covered in Chapter 7, page 87. The cost of the fruit or vegetable for any dish you prepare must include the cost of the trim, or else you will underestimate the expenses. This chapter investigates how cost is affected by the fact that you are purchasing more than you are using in a recipe.

OBJECTIVES

- Define edible portion cost and as-purchased cost.

- Calculate the edible portion cost when the as-purchased cost is given for an ingredient.

- Explain why edible portion cost will always be equal to or greater than as-purchased cost.

EDIBLE PORTION COST

Chapter 8, page 108, covered how to use the yield percent to determine how many pounds of broccoli rabe to order. Chapter 9, page 121, examined how to find the cost of ingredients that have no trim, such as flour, sugar, or dried spices. This cost is based on exactly what was used in the recipe. When you begin to find the cost of ingredients that have to be trimmed and cleaned, it is necessary to factor in the cost of the trim so that you account for your total cost. Excluding the cost of the peels, pits, cores, seeds, rinds, and/or outer leaves will result in underestimating the cost to prepare a menu item. As a result, you run the risk of undercharging for the menu item and not covering your expenses.

> **HINT**
> The edible portion cost is always greater than the as-purchased cost if the yield percent is less than 100 percent.

DEFINITIONS

AS-PURCHASED COST (APC)

The *as-purchased cost (APC)* is the cost paid to the supplier for the nonfabricated (uncleaned) ingredient.

EDIBLE PORTION COST (EPC)

The *edible portion cost (EPC)* is the cost per unit of the fabricated (cleaned) fruit or vegetable. The EPC accounts not only for the cost of the fabricated product but also for the cost of the trim.

FORMULA FOR EDIBLE PORTION COST

$$\text{Edible portion cost (EPC)} = \frac{\text{As-purchased cost (APC)}}{\text{Yield percent (in decimal form)}}$$

The following steps will allow you to calculate the edible portion cost for any ingredient that must be trimmed.

STEPS FOR CALCULATING EDIBLE PORTION COST FOR INGREDIENTS WITH LESS THAN 100% YIELD

STEP 1. Read the problem and identify the given as-purchased cost (APC) information.

STEP 2. Decide which unit to use and perform the calculations necessary to convert the as-purchased cost (APC) to this unit.

139

STEP 3. Find the yield percent (page 108).

STEP 4. Substitute the as-purchased cost (APC) and the yield percent into the edible portion cost (EPC) formula and calculate the answer.

STEP 5. Make sure the answer is reasonable.

CAUTION
The yield percent triangle shown in Chapter 7, page 91, is not designed to calculate cost. It is for calculating quantity only.

FINDING TOTAL COST

Now that we have the edible portion cost per unit, we need to apply the total cost formula from Chapter 9, page 122. The formula we use in this chapter uses different vocabulary but follows the same principles.

STEPS FOR FINDING TOTAL COST

STEP 1. Replace the number of units with the edible portion quantity.

STEP 2. Replace the cost per unit with the edible portion cost per unit.

STEP 3. Solve for the total cost.

HINT
To avoid making a mistake, pay attention to the edible portion cost number. If it is less than the as-purchased cost, something is very wrong. It will never cost less to buy a cleaned amount of anything.

TOTAL COST FORMULA

Total cost = Number of units × Cost per unit

Total cost (using EPC) = Edible portion quantity (EPQ) × Edible portion cost per unit

Use the following steps to calculate the total cost.

STEPS FOR CALCULATING TOTAL COST USING THE EDIBLE PORTION COST

STEP 1. Calculate the edible portion cost.

STEP 2. Perform the calculation necessary so that the units for edible portion *quantity* and edible portion *cost per unit* are the same.

STEP 3. Insert the numbers into the total cost formula:

Total cost = Edible portion quantity × Edible portion cost per unit

STEP 4. Round any partial pennies up to the next highest cent.

STEP 5. Check the answer to make sure it is reasonable.

In the problem from the chapter introduction, you will need 60 pounds of washed, trimmed broccoli rabe for Broccoli Rabe with Garlic and Hot Crushed Pepper. Broccoli rabe costs $1.86 per pound and has a 75 percent yield. From the information given here, we can calculate the cost of the trimmed broccoli rabe using both formulas: the edible portion cost formula and the total cost formula.

Calculating Edible Portion Cost

STEP 1. Read the problem and identify the given as-purchased cost information.

The as-purchased cost is $1.86 per pound.

STEP 2. Decide which unit of measure to use, and perform the calculations necessary to convert the as-purchased cost to the unit of choice.

In this problem, the obvious unit to stay with is pounds.

STEP 3. Find the yield percent.

The yield percent is given as 75 percent.

STEP 4. Substitute the as-purchased cost and the yield percent into the edible portion cost formula.

$$\text{EPC} = \frac{\text{APC}}{\text{Yield percent (in decimal form)}} = \frac{\$1.86 \text{ per lb}}{0.75} = \$2.48 \text{ per lb}$$

STEP 5. Make sure the answer is reasonable.

The answer, $2.48 per pound, is greater than $1.86 per pound, so it is reasonable.

Calculating Total Cost

Apply the edible portion cost to the total cost formula to find the cost of the clean broccoli rabe.

STEP 1. Calculate the edible portion cost.

$2.48 per pound

STEP 2. Make sure that the units for edible portion quantity and edible portion cost per unit are the same.

In this problem, the unit for both the quantity and the cost is pounds.

141

STEP 3. Insert the numbers into the total cost formula.

$$\text{Total cost} = \text{EPQ} \times \text{EPC per unit} = 60 \text{ lb} \times \$2.48 \text{ per lb} = \$148.80$$

STEP 4. Round any partial pennies up to the next highest cent.

This is not necessary in this problem.

STEP 5. Check the answer to make sure it is reasonable.

It makes sense that the cost of the 60 pounds of cleaned broccoli rabe is $148.80.

Note that some fruits and vegetables are available already cleaned and ready to cook and serve. When a fruit or vegetable is already cleaned, the price will include the trim loss, extra packaging, and labor, among other costs. This makes the cost of cleaned product greater than the cost of uncleaned product, even though there would be costs attached to fabricating the fruit or vegetable yourself.

EXAMPLE 2:

You are purchasing cauliflower for a party. In order to calculate the cost of the cauliflower that will be served, the cost per pound must be determined. The cauliflower was purchased by the head for $1.14. Cauliflower has a 45 percent yield, and each head weighs 2 pounds. What is the edible portion cost per pound?

STEP 1. Read the problem and identify the given as-purchased cost information.

The as-purchased cost is $1.14 per head.

STEP 2. Decide which unit of measure to use, and perform the calculations necessary to convert the as-purchased cost to this unit.

The problem asks for the cost per pound, so use the cost per unit formula to calculate the cost per pound for the cauliflower.

$$\text{Cost per unit} = \frac{\text{As-purchased cost}}{\text{Number of units}} = \frac{\$1.14}{2 \text{ lb}} = \$0.57 \text{ per lb}$$

STEP 3. Find the yield percent.

The yield percent for cauliflower is given in the problem as 45 percent.

142

STEP 4. Substitute the as-purchased cost and the yield percent into the edible portion cost formula and calculate the answer.

$$\text{EPC} = \frac{\text{APC}}{\text{Yield percent (in decimal form)}} = \frac{\$0.57 \text{ per lb}}{0.45} = \$1.2666 \text{ per lb, or } \$1.27 \text{ per lb}$$

STEP 5. Make sure the answer is reasonable.

The result, $1.27 per pound of cleaned cauliflower, does make sense, as it is appropriately higher than $0.57 per pound.

In the problem above, it is not necessary to calculate the total cost because the question asks only for the edible portion cost for 1 pound.

EXAMPLE 3:

You are making a pesto sauce for a chicken dish you are preparing. You purchase basil in bunches. Each bunch weighs 2 ½ ounces and costs $0.79. One tablespoon of cleaned, chopped basil weighs 0.09 ounce, and basil has a 56 percent yield. How much will 1 cup of cleaned, chopped basil cost for this recipe?

Calculating Edible Portion Cost

STEP 1. Read the problem and identify the given as-purchased cost information.

Basil is bought by the bunch for $0.79.

STEP 2. Decide which unit of measure to use and perform the calculations necessary to convert the as-purchased cost to this unit. Because the weight is given in ounces, it is wise to stick with this unit and avoid unnecessary conversions.

$$\text{Cost per unit} = \frac{\text{As-purchased cost}}{\text{Number of units}} = \frac{\$0.79}{2.5 \text{ oz}} = \$0.316 \text{ per oz}$$

STEP 3. Find the yield percent.

The yield percent is given in the problem: 56 percent.

STEP 4. Substitute the as-purchased cost and the yield percent into the edible portion cost formula and calculate the answer.

$$\text{Edible portion cost} = \frac{\text{As-purchased cost}}{\text{Yield percent (in decimal form)}} = \frac{\$0.316 \text{ per oz}}{0.56} = \$0.5642 \text{ per oz}$$

STEP 5. Make sure that the answer is reasonable.

The edible portion cost, $0.5642 per ounce, is greater than the cost per unit, $0.316 per ounce, so it makes sense.

Calculating Total Cost

STEP 1. Calculate the edible portion cost.

We calculated the edible portion cost of the basil as $0.5642 per ounce.

STEP 2. Perform the calculations necessary so that the edible portion quantity and the edible portion cost per unit have the same unit. The cost is per ounce, so, using the bridge method (Chapter 4, page 50), convert the cup of basil to ounces.

$$\frac{1 \ \cancel{\text{cup}}}{1} \times \frac{16 \ \text{tbsp}}{1 \ \cancel{\text{cup}}} = \frac{16 \ \cancel{\text{tbsp}}}{1} \times \frac{0.09 \ \text{oz}}{1 \ \cancel{\text{tbsp}}} = 1.44 \ \text{oz}$$

STEP 3. Substitute the numbers into the total cost formula.

$$\begin{aligned} \text{Total cost} &= \text{EPQ} \times \text{EPC per unit} \\ &= 1.44 \ \text{oz} \times \$0.5642 \ \text{per oz} = \$0.8124 \end{aligned}$$

STEP 4. Round any partial pennies up to the next highest cent.

The cost of the cup of chopped fresh basil is $0.8124, or $0.82.

STEP 5. Check the answer to make sure it is reasonable.

Since an ounce of chopped fresh basil costs $0.5642, it makes sense that 1.44 ounces costs a bit more.

INGREDIENTS WITH 100 PERCENT YIELD

In addition to those shown below, many products have 100 percent yield, such as flour, sugar, dried spices, wines, spirits, syrups, and processed foods. The edible portion cost may still be computed for these products, but we would be dividing by 1 (the decimal form of 100 percent), and any number divided by 1 equals itself. As a result, the edible portion cost and the as-purchased cost are the same.

For example, a jar of chili powder costs $5.15 per pound. A jar holds 1 pound. This entire product is usable, which makes the yield percent 100 percent. In order to find the edible

(continues on page 146)

FINDING THE COST OF MEAT AND POULTRY

When determining the cost of the meat or poultry that you fabricate, the terminology changes. For meat and poultry, we use the terms *new fabricated cost* and *new fabricated price per pound* instead of *edible portion cost*. The new fabricated price per pound recognizes the value of the trim that resulted from the fabrication process.

$$\text{New fabricated price per pound} = \frac{\text{New fabricated cost}}{\text{New fabricated weight}}$$

In the butcher's yield test from Chapter 7, page 96, you purchased a rib that weighs 36.9 pounds. The fat weighed 8 pounds, the bones weighed 7.3 pounds, and the usable trim weighed 8.7 pounds. The entire rib was originally purchased for $2.03 per pound. In Chapter 7, the new fabricated weight was calculated to be 12.9 pounds. The as-purchased cost is calculated by multiplying the as-purchased weight by the as-purchased price per pound:

36.9 lb × $2.03 per lb = $74.91

STEP 1. To determine the value of the trim, check the current market prices with your purveyor. The following example is based on the following prices:

> Fat: $0.02 per pound
> Bones: $0.46 per pound
> Usable trim: $2.45 per pound

STEP 2. The total trim value is calculated by multiplying the price per pound by the number of pounds of each type of trim.

> | | | |
> |---|---|---|
> | Fat: | $0.02/lb × 8.0 lb = | $ 0.16 |
> | Bones: | $0.46/lb × 7.3 lb = | $ 3.36 |
> | Usable trim: | $2.45/lb × 8.7 lb = | $21.32 |
> | Total trim value: | | $24.84 |

STEP 3. To determine the new fabricated cost, subtract the total trim value from the as-purchased cost:

> $74.91 − $24.84 = $50.07

STEP 4. To determine the new fabricated price per pound, substitute the new fabricated cost ($50.07) and the new fabricated weight (12.9 pounds) into the formula:

$$\text{New fabricated price per pound} = \frac{\text{New fabricated cost}}{\text{New fabricated weight}} = \frac{\$50.07}{12.9}$$

$$= \$3.89 \text{ per lb}$$

This is the price you would use if you were costing a recipe with this particular fabricated meat as an ingredient.

145

Examples of ingredients with 100 percent yield include sugars, dairy, spirits, seasonings, special baking items, and pasta.

portion cost, you would divide $5.15 by 1 (the decimal form of 100 percent). Consequently, the edible portion cost ($5.15 per pound) and the as-purchased cost ($5.15 per pound) are the same.

HINT

When the yield is 100 percent, the as-purchased cost and the edible portion cost will be equal.

CHAPTER REVIEW

There is a substantial amount of math involved in calculating the cost of ingredients that you will be using in recipes. It is imperative that you master this skill so that you may correctly determine the costs of your menu items and ultimately their selling prices.

FORMULA FOR EDIBLE PORTION COST

$$\text{Edible portion cost (EPC)} = \frac{\text{As-purchased cost (APC)}}{\text{Yield percent (in decimal form)}}$$

146

STEPS FOR CALCULATING THE TOTAL COST USING THE EDIBLE PORTION COST

STEP 1. Calculate the edible portion cost.

STEP 2. Perform the calculations necessary so that the units for edible portion *quantity* and edible portion *cost per unit* are the same.

STEP 3. Insert the numbers into the total cost formula:

$$\text{Total cost} = \text{EPQ} \times \text{EPC per unit}$$

STEP 4. Round any partial pennies up to the next highest cent.

STEP 5. Check the answer to make sure it is reasonable.

CHAPTER PRACTICE

Answers to odd-numbered questions may be found on page 252.

Calculate the edible portion cost (EPC) per pound for the following items. For items marked with a star (*), find the average weight per each item before solving. See the Approximate Yield of Fruits and Vegetables Chart on page 95.

Item	APC	Yield %	EPC per Pound
1. Mustard greens	$0.53/lb	75	_____
2. Pineapples*	$2.93/ea	52	_____
3. Eggplant	$1.12/lb	84	_____
4. Coconut*	$0.50/ea	53	_____
5. Celery*	$0.62/bunch	75	_____
6. Leeks*	$1.45/bunch	52	_____

7. You need 4.5 pounds of cleaned lettuce to make enough salad for a party of 20 people. Each head weighs 2.25 pounds and the yield percent is 74 percent. A head of lettuce costs $0.59. What is the cost of the lettuce for this party?

_____

_____

_____

_____

_____

8. For a dessert you are making, you have purchased 4 pounds of raspberries at $3.29 per pound. When you prepare the raspberries, you have a 3 percent trim loss. How much would 1 pound of cleaned raspberries cost?

_____

_____

_____

_____

_____

9. You have received new potatoes in the produce delivery. The as-purchased cost of the potatoes is $0.75 per pound. If the yield on the potatoes is 81 percent, what is the edible portion cost per pound?

_____

_____

_____

_____

10. Chef Alice made 27 Blueberry Crêpes for a party. Each crêpe contained 5 ounces of cleaned blueberries. The yield percent for blueberries is 92 percent. If Chef Alice bought blueberries in season for $1.80 per pound, how much would the blueberries cost for the party?

_____

_____

_____

_____

11. You purchase 3 pounds of fresh lychee nuts for $12.45 and the yield is 60 percent. What is the edible portion cost per pound for the fresh lychee nuts?

_____

_____

_____

_____

_____

12. The yield for strawberries is 87 percent. A pint of strawberries costs $1.92. How much would 1 cup of cleaned strawberries cost?

_____

_____

_____

_____

_____

13. How much will 8 pints of cleaned raspberries cost if the as-purchased cost is $3.29 per pound? One cup of cleaned raspberries weighs 4.5 ounces and has a yield percent of 97 percent.

_____

_____

_____

_____

_____

14. You have just received 50 pounds of russet potatoes. The invoice lists a price of $29.50 for 50 pounds of potatoes. If the yield percent on russet potatoes is 81 percent, what is the edible portion cost for 1 pound?

_____

_____

_____

_____

_____

15. You have decided to use fresh shredded coconut for Toasted Coconut Ice Cream. You will need 170 grams of shredded coconut to make 1.5 liters of ice cream. One cup of shredded coconut weighs $2\frac{1}{2}$ ounces. The yield for coconut is 53 percent, and each coconut weighs approximately 26 ounces. Coconuts are purchased for $0.55 each. How much will the 170 grams of fresh shredded coconut cost?

_____

_____

_____

_____

_____

16. A recipe for Banana Pie calls for 5 ½ cups of peeled, diced bananas. If bananas are purchased for $0.59 per pound, how much will the 5 ½ cups cost?

_____

_____

_____

_____

_____

17. Why is the EPC always equal to or higher than the APC? Give an example of when they are equal.

_____

_____

_____

_____

_____

18. You are making freshly squeezed orange juice for a brunch you are catering. You need to make 3 liters of orange juice. Oranges are purchased by the case for $24. Each case contains 100 oranges. Each orange weighs 6 ½ ounces and has a yield percent, for juicing, of 50%. What is the edible portion cost for the orange juice for this brunch?

_____

_____

_____

_____

_____

19. You purchase a case of mangos for $9.89. The case weighs 4.1 kilograms. The recipe for Mango Gazpacho calls for 4 ½ cups of roughly chopped mango. The yield percent for mangos is 68 percent and 1 cup of roughly chopped mango weighs 5.9 ounces. How much will the mangos for this recipe cost?

_____

_____

_____

_____

_____

20. You are making Lemon Sorbet. Lemons are purchased by the case. A case of lemons contains 50 lemons and sells for $16.50. Each lemon weighs 4 ounces. The yield percent for lemon juice is 41 percent. How many lemons will you use to make 1.75 liters of lemon juice, and how much will it cost?

_____

_____

_____

_____

_____

21. A recipe for Sweet Cherry Pie calls for 1 ½ quarts of pitted sweet cherries. The yield percent for cherries is 87 percent. One cup of pitted sweet cherries weighs 5 ¼ ounces. Cherries are purchased in 10-pound cases for $19.90. How much will the sweet cherries for this pie cost?

_____

_____

_____

_____

_____

22. You can purchase a pound of _cleaned_ romaine lettuce for $1.69. You can also purchase 1 whole head of _uncleaned_ romaine lettuce for $0.99. The whole head of romaine lettuce weighs 24 ounces. The yield percent on romaine lettuce is 75 percent. What is the difference in the cost per pound between these two forms of romaine lettuce? Are there any other considerations that need to be taken into account when choosing between cleaned and uncleaned romaine lettuce?

_____

_____

_____

_____

_____

23. Jalapeños are purchased for $1.69 a pound. The yield percent is 86 percent. How much would 5 ounces of clean jalapeños cost?

_____

_____

_____

_____

_____

151

24. Cilantro is purchased by the pound. There are 6 bunches in 1 pound. You purchase cilantro for $8.94 a pound. If 1 cup of cilantro weighs 1.4 ounces and the yield percent for cilantro is 42 percent, how much would 1 teaspoon of clean cilantro cost?

_____

_____

_____

_____

_____

25. You are making Ginger Sweet Potato Salad. The recipe calls for 6 pounds 3 ounces of cleaned, cubed sweet potatoes. You purchase sweet potatoes in 50-pound bags for $34.00. The yield percent for sweet potatoes is 75 percent. How much will the sweet potatoes cost for this recipe?

_____

_____

_____

_____

26. You are serving Pork with Sautéed Apple Slices to 125 guests. Each serving requires 1.5 ounces of peeled, cored, sliced apples. Apples are purchased by the case, 50 apples to a case. Each apple weighs approximately 8 ounces. A case of apples costs $30.75. How much will the apples cost for the party if the yield percent for apples is 85 percent?

_____

_____

_____

_____

27. A recipe for Fresh Mango Chutney calls for 2 pounds of small diced mango. Mangos are purchased by the each for $1.53. Each mango weighs approximately 11 ounces and has a yield of 68%. How much will the mango for this recipe cost?

_____

_____

_____

_____

_____

152

28. You have a recipe that calls for 2 ½ cups of celery. One cup of celery weighs 4 ounces, and celery has a yield percent of 68 percent. If celery costs $0.77 per bunch and a bunch weighs 2 pounds, then how much will the celery for this recipe cost?

_____

_____

_____

_____

_____

29. You are catering a garden party for 80 guests and serving Watercress Sandwiches with Herb Mayonnaise. The recipe calls or 1 ½ pounds of cleaned, trimmed watercress. Watercress is purchased by the bunch for $0.56. A bunch of watercress weighs 7 ounces and has a yield of 30%. How much will the watercress cost for this recipe?

_____

_____

_____

_____

_____

30. You are making Cold Poached Salmon with Rice. The recipe calls for ¾ cup of onions. A cup of onion weighs 6.5 ounces and costs $0.55 per pound. How much will the onions cost for this recipe?

_____

_____

_____

_____

_____

31. You need 3 grams of fresh, chopped dill for Cucumber Sandwiches with Herbed Cream Cheese. The yield for dill is 44 percent. Dill is purchased by the bunch for $0.85 and weighs 4 ½ ounces. How much will the dill cost for this recipe?

_____

_____

_____

_____

_____

153

Recipe Costing

11

Chef Jean-Jacques opened a restaurant last year. The food was excellent, and it was busy every night. Unfortunately, the restaurant closed eight months after it opened. What happened? An examination of the books revealed that the food was costing Jean-Jacques more than he thought, and unfortunately, he was not charging enough. Although the food was delicious and there were many loyal customers, Jean-Jacques did not control costs sufficiently, and the business could not survive. Excellence in the culinary arts is only one of the many skills necessary to be successful in the food-service industry. One must also recognize the importance of the skills required to make a profit.

This chapter examines recipe costing, which is the process of calculating the cost of the ingredients in a recipe and is the basis of good food cost control. It is safe to say that all of the chapters leading up to this chapter are to prepare you to master recipe costing. This skill is as important as mastering cooking techniques for your success in the food-service industry.

OBJECTIVES

- State the major reasons for a strong recipe precosting program.
- Identify the components of a food cost form.
- Cost out a recipe by completing a food cost form correctly.
- Calculate the cost to produce a given recipe and the cost per portion.
- Calculate an estimated selling price given an estimated food cost percent.

FOOD COST

The term *food cost* refers to the total cost of food items used in food production. Food cost does not include utensils, fuel for cooking, water, utilities, labor, or supplies. Food cost may be expressed as the cost of any of the following:

- A single item, such as a steak, a portion of fish, or a vegetable

- A single recipe, such as an entrée, soup, sauce, salad, bread, or cake

- Several items that make up a complete plate, such as a steak with potato, vegetable, and garnish

- Several components of a complete meal, such as bread and butter, soup, salad, entrée, dessert, and beverage

- Food items for a specific time period, such as breakfast, lunch, dinner, a day, a week, or a year

Any of the above examples may also be expressed in relation to the selling price of the item or the total food sales for a given period.

DETERMINING FOOD COST PERCENT

The food cost percent is the percent of the selling price that pays for the ingredients. The formula for the food cost percent is

$$\text{Food cost percent} = \frac{\text{Food cost}}{\text{Food sales}} \text{ or } \frac{\text{Cost per portion}}{\text{Selling price}}$$

For example, the cost per portion of beef stew is $0.92, and you are charging $4.00 per serving. Calculate the food cost percent as follows:

$$\text{Food cost percent} = \frac{\text{Cost per portion}}{\text{Selling price}} = \frac{\$0.92}{\$4.00} = 0.23 \text{ or } 23\%$$

This indicates that 23 percent of the sales for beef stew pays for ingredients used to make it. What happens to the other 77 percent? The sales must also pay for the other expenses the operation incurred producing the beef stew: labor, utilities, and rent. Any remaining sales become profit.

Another way of looking at food cost is to relate it to a dollar. If a recipe has a 40 percent food cost, it may be said that the food cost is $0.40 for each $1.00 of sales.

The food cost percent for an operation is a very important number. It is one of the tools used by management to evaluate profitability and menu items. Food cost for individual recipes, which is what this book examines, has two primary purposes for management: determining the selling price and forming the basis for a strong cost control program.

DETERMINING SELLING PRICE USING FOOD COST PERCENT

Once you have calculated how much a recipe costs to make, the cost per portion can be calculated with the following formula:

$$\text{Cost per portion} = \frac{\text{Total recipe cost}}{\text{Number of portions}}$$

The cost per portion is then used to calculate the selling price based on a desired food cost percent:

$$\text{Selling price} = \frac{\text{Cost per portion}}{\text{Food cost percent (in decimal form)}}$$

There are many different ways to calculate the selling price for a menu item. The method addressed in this textbook is related to the mathematical formulas above. Other resources approach selling price from different avenues. These different methods should be researched before choosing menu prices. Oftentimes a restaurant will determine the desired food cost percent based on a projected budget. The chef will then use this food cost percent to determine the selling price.

THE COST PER PORTION, SELLING PRICE, AND FOOD COST PERCENT TRIANGLE

The following triangle is a tool used to find the cost per portion, selling price, and food cost percent. It is identical to the Percent Triangle introduced in Chapter 1, page 12, although the application differs.

PART = Cost per portion

WHOLE = Selling price

PERCENT = Food cost percent

STEPS FOR USING THE COST PER PORTION, SELLING PRICE, AND FOOD COST PERCENT TRIANGLE

STEP 1. Determine what you are looking for: cost per portion, selling price, or food cost percent.

STEP 2. *To find the cost per portion*
Cover the cost per portion in the triangle.

Selling price and food cost percent are side by side. This directs you to multiply the selling

price by the food cost percent. (Remember to change the percent to a decimal by dividing by 100 before multiplying.)

To find the selling price
Cover the selling price in the triangle.

Cost per portion is over food cost percent. This directs you to divide the cost per portion by the food cost percent. (Remember to change the percent to a decimal by dividing by 100 before multiplying.)

To find the food cost percent
Cover the food cost percent in the triangle.

Cost per portion is over selling price. This directs you to divide the cost per portion by the selling price and multiply the answer by 100 to convert it to the food cost percent.

COST CONTROL: KEEPING DOWN THE COST PER PORTION

Cost control is the process used to regulate cost and guard against excessive cost. You should determine food cost through the use of food cost forms (described later in this chapter) and compare it to the actual food cost, which is based on inventory. This offers a good opportunity to make sure that the operation is running efficiently. If any discrepancies are found, you can examine the situation and make the appropriate changes.

THE ARITHMETIC OF RECIPE COSTING

To arrive at an accurate cost of any menu item before it is produced, a standard recipe listing the ingredients and amounts, as well as the number of portions or servings desired, must be established. In addition, the following information must also be available:

1. The purchase unit and current market price of the ingredients (usually obtained from the supplier)

2. The yield percent, to convert the as-purchased cost (APC) to the edible portion cost (EPC) (see the Approximate Yield of Fruits and Vegetables Chart on page 95)

3. Volume to weight conversion formulas, to convert the ingredient's units and the purchase units when they do not correspond (see the Approximate Volume to Weight Chart on page 74)

The form on the next page is an example of a blank food cost form.

157

FOOD COST FORM

Menu Item: _____ Date: _____

Number of Portions: _____ Size: _____

Cost per Portion: _____ Selling Price: _____ Food Cost %: _____

Ingredients	Recipe Quantity (EP)			Cost			Total Cost
	Weight	Volume	Count	APC/Unit	Yield %	EPC/Unit	
					TOTAL RECIPE COST		

CALCULATING RECIPE COST

The total cost formula was examined in Chapter 10, page 140. This formula can be directly applied to the food cost form. Once again, the edible portion quantity and the as-purchased cost or edible portion cost must be converted to the same unit before multiplying them to calculate the total cost. Remember that this is only one method for finding the total cost of each ingredient and that there are other possibilities. However, even if the math is done differently, your answer should be exactly the same. Once you have mastered the steps for calculating cost on a food cost form, you can use the interactive Excel food cost form at http://www.wiley.com/go/culinarymath for additional practice.

STEPS FOR CALCULATING TOTAL COST ON A FOOD COST FORM

STEP 1. Look at the units in each row, one row at a time, and decide what units to use to solve the problem.

STEP 2. Convert the edible portion quantity and the as-purchased cost to the chosen unit.

STEP 3. Calculate the edible portion cost using the as-purchased cost and the yield percent, if necessary.

STEP 4. Substitute the edible portion quantity and the edible portion cost per unit into the total cost formula.

$$\text{Total cost} = \text{EPQ} \times \text{EPC per unit}$$

Must be the same unit

STEP 5. Round any partial pennies up to the next highest cent.

STEP 6. Make sure that the total cost for each ingredient makes sense.

ELEMENTS ON A FOOD COST FORM

MENU ITEM: The name of the recipe identified as accurately as possible, using a menu number if necessary.

DATE: The day, month, and year the cost was calculated. This can be important for later analysis.

NUMBER OF PORTIONS: The number of portions the recipe makes or yields.

SIZE: The portion size normally served. This applies to menu items and is generally given in the recipe; it is not calculated.

COST PER PORTION: The cost of each serving. It is the total recipe cost divided by the number of portions.

SELLING PRICE: Based on the food cost percent allowed by the budget. It is the cost per portion divided by the food cost percent (in decimal form).

$$\text{Selling price} = \frac{\text{Cost per portion}}{\text{Food cost percent (in decimal form)}}$$

FOOD COST %: An expression of food cost in relation to the selling price. It is the cost per portion divided by the selling price.

$$\text{Food cost percent} = \frac{\text{Cost per portion}}{\text{Selling price}}$$

INGREDIENTS: All the food items that make up the recipe, including specific sizes or ID numbers.

RECIPE QUANTITY: This will be listed by weight, volume, or count, depending on the recipe. The recipe quantity is usually the edible portion quantity. There are exceptions to this, which will be addressed in Chapter 12, page 176. Recipe quantity is recorded in one of three ways.

1. By weight—pounds, ounces, grams, etc.

2. By volume—cups, pints, tablespoons, etc.

3. By count—each, bunch, case, etc.

APC/UNIT: The as-purchased cost per unit is the current market price or the as-purchased price and the unit upon which price is based.

YIELD %: Many foods are not purchased already cleaned, and with these, some waste (trim) is expected. The yield percent is used to adjust the as-purchased cost to compensate for trim loss.

EPC/UNIT: Edible portion cost per unit is the cost per unit of the fabricated fruit or vegetable. This cost accounts not only for the cost of the fabricated product but also for the trim loss. This is calculated by dividing the APC by the yield percent (see Chapter 10, page 139).

$$\text{EPC} = \frac{\text{APC per unit}}{\text{Yield percent (in decimal form)}}$$

If there is no waste or trim, the yield is 100 percent and this column may be left blank.

TOTAL COST: The total cost of each ingredient used.

TOTAL RECIPE COST: The sum of all items in the total cost column. This represents the total estimated cost of the recipe.

STEPS FOR CALCULATING THE TOTAL RECIPE COST, COST PER PORTION, AND SELLING PRICE ON A FOOD COST FORM

STEP 1. Find the sum of the costs of all ingredients.

STEP 2. Find the cost per portion by dividing the total recipe cost by the number of portions.

$$\text{Cost per portion} = \frac{\text{Total recipe cost}}{\text{Number of portions}}$$

STEP 3. Determine the selling price by dividing the cost per portion by the food cost percent.

$$\text{Selling price} = \frac{\text{Cost per portion}}{\text{Food cost percent (in decimal form)}}$$

EXAMPLE:

FOOD COST FORM

Menu Item: Grilled Herbed Salmon   Date:

Number of Portions: 10   Size:

Cost per Portion: Selling Price: Food Cost %: 30%

Ingredients	Recipe Quantity (EP)			Cost			Total Cost
	Weight	Volume	Count	APC/Unit	Yield %	EPC/Unit	
1. Salmon filet	2¼ lb			$5.54/lb	100		
2. Lime juice (1 ea = 2.2 oz)		2 tbsp		$0.14/ea	35		
3. Parsley, chopped (1 bunch = 0.33 lb) (1 cup = 1 oz)		2 tbsp		$0.49/ bunch	76		
4. Chives, chopped (1 bunch = 1 oz) (1 tbsp = 0.1 oz)		2 tbsp		$0.67/ bunch	100		
5. Thyme, chopped (1 bunch = 1 oz) (1 tbsp = 0.1 oz)		1 tbsp		$0.46/ bunch	65		
6. Black peppercorn, crushed (jar = 1 lb) (1 tbsp = 0.25 oz)		2 tsp		$9.11/jar	100		
						TOTAL RECIPE COST	

162

CULINARY MATH

SOLUTION

FOOD COST FORM

Menu Item: Grilled Herbed Salmon   Date:

Number of Portions: 10   Size:

Cost per Portion: Selling Price: Food Cost %: 30%

Ingredients	Recipe Quantity (EP)			Cost			Total
	Weight	Volume	Count	APC/Unit	Yield %	EPC/Unit	**Cost**
1. Salmon filet	2¼ lb			$5.54/lb	100		$12.47
Solution using pounds: 2.25 lb × $5.54/lb = $12.465, or $12.47							
2. Lime juice (1 ea = 2.2 oz)		2 tbsp		$0.14/each	35		$0.19
Solution: 1 lime weighs 2.2 ounces. 1 tablespoon of lime juice weighs ½ ounce. Convert this row to ounces. $\dfrac{2\ \text{tbsp}}{1} \times \dfrac{0.5\ \text{oz}}{1\ \text{tbsp}} = 1\ \text{oz}$ $\dfrac{\$0.14}{2.2\ \text{oz}} = \$0.0636/\text{oz (APC)}$ $\dfrac{\$0.0636/\text{oz (APC)}}{0.35} = \$0.1818/\text{oz (EPC)}$ 1 oz × $0.1818/oz = $0.1818, or $0.19							
3. Parsley, chopped (1 bunch = 0.33 lb) (1 cup = 1 oz)		2 tbsp		$0.49/ bunch	76		$0.02
Solution: Convert this row to ounces using the given information. $\dfrac{2\ \text{tbsp}}{1} \times \dfrac{1\ \text{cup}}{16\ \text{tbsp}} = \dfrac{0.125\ \text{cup}}{1} \times \dfrac{1\ \text{oz}}{1\ \text{cup}} = 0.125\ \text{oz}$ $\dfrac{\$0.49}{0.33\ \text{lb}} = \$1.4848/\text{lb} = \$0.0928/\text{oz (APC)}$ $\dfrac{\$0.0928}{0.76} = \$0.1221/\text{oz (EPC)}$ 0.125 oz × $0.1221/oz = $0.0152, or $0.02							
4. Chives, chopped (1 bunch = 1 oz) (1 tbsp = 0.1 oz)		2 tbsp		$0.67/ bunch	100		$0.14

163

Solution: Both bunch and tablespoons can be converted to ounces.						
$\dfrac{2\ \cancel{tbsp}}{1} \times \dfrac{0.1\ oz}{1\ \cancel{tbsp}} = 0.2\ oz \qquad \dfrac{\$0.67}{1\ oz} = \$0.67/oz$						
$0.2\ oz \times \$0.67/oz = \$0.134,\ or\ \$0.14$						
5. Thyme, chopped (1 bunch = 1 oz) (1 tbsp = 0.1 oz)		1 tbsp	$0.46/ bunch	65		$0.08
Solution: The weight of a tablespoon and the bunch is given in ounces.						
1 tbsp = 0.1 oz $0.46/bunch (1 oz) (APC)						
$\dfrac{\$0.46}{0.65} = \$0.7076/oz\ (EPC)$						
$0.1\ oz \times \$0.7076/oz = \$0.0707,\ or\ \$0.08$						
6. Black peppercorn, crushed (jar = 1 lb) (1 tbsp = 0.25 oz)		2 tsp	$9.11/jar	100		$0.10
Solution: The weight of the tablespoon is in ounces and the weight of the jar is in pounds. It would be reasonable to convert to ounces or pounds. For this example, convert the teaspoons to pounds and leave the APC alone.						
$\dfrac{2\ \cancel{tsp}}{1} \times \dfrac{1\ tbsp}{3\ \cancel{tsp}} = \dfrac{0.6666\ \cancel{tbsp}}{1} \times \dfrac{0.25\ oz}{1\ \cancel{tbsp}} = \dfrac{0.1666\ \cancel{oz}}{1} \times \dfrac{1\ lb}{16\ \cancel{oz}} = 0.0104\ lb$						
$0.0104\ lb \times \$9.11/lb = \$0.0948,\ or\ \$0.10$						
Add all the total costs to find the total recipe cost.						
TOTAL RECIPE COST						$13.00

FOOD COST FORM

Menu Item: Grilled Herbed Salmon   Date:

Number of Portions: 10   Size:

Cost per Portion: *1.30*   Selling Price: *4.34*   Food Cost %: 30%

Ingredients	Recipe Quantity (EP)			Cost			Total
	Weight	Volume	Count	APC/Unit	Yield %	EPC/Unit	Cost
1. Salmon filet	2¼ lb *2.25 lb*			$5.54/lb	100	*$5.54/lb*	*12.47*
2. Lime juice (1 ea = 2.2 oz)	$\frac{2}{1} \times \frac{0.5\ oz}{1} = 1\ oz$	2 tbsp		$0.14 oz/ea $\frac{\$0.14}{2.2\ oz} = \$.0636\ oz$	35	*$0.1818/oz*	*0.19*
3. Parsley, chopped (1 bunch = 0.33 lb) (1 cup = 1 oz)	*0.125 oz* $\frac{2\ tbsp}{1} \times \frac{1c}{16\ tbsp} = \frac{0.125\ c}{1}$	2 tbsp		$0.49/ bunch $\times \frac{1\ oz}{1\ c}$ $\frac{0.49}{33\ lb} = \frac{\$1.4848\ lb}{16\ oz} = \frac{\$0.0928}{0.76}$	76	*$0.1221/oz*	*0.02*
4. Chives, chopped (1 bunch = 1 oz) (1 tbsp = 0.1 oz)	$\frac{2\ tpsp}{1} \times \frac{0.1\ oz}{1\ tbsp} = 0.2\ oz$	2 tbsp		$0.67/oz	100	*$0.67/oz*	*0.14*
5. Thyme, chopped (1 bunch = 1 oz) (1 tbsp = 0.1 oz)		1 tbsp *0.1 oz*		$0.46/oz	65	*$0.7076/ oz*	*0.08*
6. Black peppercorn, crushed (jar = 1 lb) (1 tbsp = 0.25 oz)	$\frac{2\ tsp}{1} \times \frac{1\ tbsp}{3\ tsp} = \frac{0.6666\ tbsp}{1} \times \frac{0.25\ oz}{1}$	2 tsp		$9.11/1 lb	100	*$3.11/lb*	*0.10*
	$\frac{0.1666}{1} \times \frac{1\ lb}{16} = 0.0104\ lb$						
						TOTAL RECIPE COST	*13.00*

Handwritten food cost form

165

To calculate the cost per portion, substitute the numbers into the formula:

$$\text{Cost per portion} = \frac{\text{Total recipe cost}}{\text{Number of portions}} = \frac{\$13.00}{10} = \$1.30 \text{ per portion}$$

To determine selling price using the given food cost percent, insert the numbers into the formula:

$$\text{Selling price} = \frac{\text{Cost per portion}}{\text{Food cost percent}} = \frac{\$1.30}{0.30} = \$4.3333, \text{ or } \$4.34$$

CHAPTER REVIEW

Recipe costing is a critical part of the success that can be achieved in the food-service industry. Knowing the total cost, cost per portion, and selling price of menu items will give you a tremendous advantage over your competitors, as well as an opportunity to manage your costs. When costing out recipes in the food-service industry you will start with a blank food cost form and will have to gather all of the information that is already conveniently gathered for you in this textbook. Knowing when and where to find this information is an important part of recipe costing.

This chapter is a culmination of the previous chapters. If you find you need more practice in any of the aspects of food costing found in this chapter, you should go back to and review the appropriate chapter(s). You can also access an interactive Excel food cost form at http://www.wiley.com/go/culinarymath for further practice in recipe costing.

DETERMINING FOOD COST PERCENT

The food cost percent is the percent of the selling price that pays for the ingredients. The formula for the food cost percent is

$$\text{Food cost percent} = \frac{\text{Food cost}}{\text{Food sales}} \text{ or } \frac{\text{Cost per portion}}{\text{Selling price}}$$

DETERMINING COST PER PORTION

The cost per portion can be calculated with the following formula:

$$\text{Cost per portion} = \frac{\text{Total recipe cost}}{\text{Number of portions}}$$

DETERMINING SELLING PRICE

The cost per portion is used to calculate the selling price based on a desired food cost percent.

$$\text{Selling price} = \frac{\text{Cost per portion}}{\text{Food cost percent (in decimal form)}}$$

THE COST PER PORTION, SELLING PRICE, AND FOOD COST PERCENT TRIANGLE

The following triangle is a tool used to find the cost per portion, selling price, and food cost percent. It is identical to the Percent Triangle introduced in Chapter 1, page 12, although the application differs.

PART = Cost per portion

WHOLE = Selling price

PERCENT = Food cost percent

STEPS FOR USING THE COST PER PORTION, SELLING PRICE, AND FOOD COST PERCENT TRIANGLE

STEP 1. Determine what you are looking for: cost per portion, selling price, or food cost percent.

STEP 2. *To find the cost per portion*
Cover the cost per portion in the triangle.

Selling price and food cost percent are side by side. This directs you to multiply the selling price by the food cost percent. (Remember to change the percent to a decimal by dividing by 100 before multiplying.)

To find the selling price
Cover the selling price in the triangle.

Cost per portion is over food cost percent. This directs you to divide the cost per portion by the food cost percent. (Remember to change the percent to a decimal by dividing by 100 before multiplying.)

To find the food cost percent
Cover the food cost percent in the triangle.

Cost per portion is over selling price. This directs you to divide the cost per portion by the selling price and multiply the answer by 100 to convert it to the food cost percent.

CHAPTER PRACTICE

Answers to odd-numbered questions may be found on page 251.
Complete the following food cost forms to determine the total recipe cost, the cost per portion, and the selling price.

167

FOOD COST FORM 1

Menu Item: New Mexican Green Chili Stew   Date:

Number of Portions: 10   Size:

Cost per Portion: Selling Price: Food Cost %: 25%

Ingredients	Recipe Quantity (EP)			Cost			Total
	Weight	Volume	Count	APC/Unit	Yield %	EPC/Unit	Cost
1. White beans, dried	8 oz			$0.40/lb	100		
2. Pork shoulder, medium dice	3½ lb			$1.49/lb	100		
3. Chicken stock		2½ qt		$6.00/gal	100		
4. Anaheim peppers	19 oz			$2.01/lb	80		
5. Vegetable oil		2 tbsp		$6.06/gal	100		
6. Onions, diced	12 oz			$0.35/lb	89		
7. Garlic, minced	1 oz			$1.89/lb	88		
8. Potatoes	2 lb			$0.41/lb	85		
9. Cilantro, chopped 1 bunch = 2.8 oz	2¾ oz			$0.45/ bunch	74		
10. Salt 1 cup = 10.5 oz		1 tbsp		$0.38/ 1 lb 10 oz	100		
11. Jalapeños, seeded and chopped	1½ oz			$1.59/lb	81		
						TOTAL RECIPE COST	

FOOD COST FORM 2

Menu Item: Ranch Dressing   Date:

Number of Portions: 32   Size:

Cost per Portion: Selling Price: Food Cost %: 15%

Ingredients	Recipe Quantity (EP)			Cost			Total Cost
	Weight	Volume	Count	APC/Unit	Yield %	EPC/Unit	
1. Sour cream		1½ cups		$0.81/pt	100		
2. Mayonnaise		1½ cups		$7.88/gal	100		
3. Buttermilk		8 fl oz		$0.63/pt	100		
4. Lemon juice 1 ea = 3.5 oz		1 fl oz		$0.18/ea	45		
5. Red wine vinegar		2 fl oz		$1.82/ 32 fl oz	100		
6. Garlic, minced 1 cup = 4.6 oz		2 tsp		$1.73/lb	87		
7. Worcester-shire sauce		3 tbsp		$1.10/5 fl oz	100		
8. Parsley, minced 1 cup = 1 oz 1 bunch = 0.33 lb		1 tbsp		$0.49/ bunch	76		
9. Chives, snipped 1 cup = 2.5 oz		1 tbsp		$2.25/lb	98		
10. Shallots 1 tbsp = 0.4 oz		1 tbsp		$1.01/lb	90		
11. Dijon mustard 1 cup = 8.5 oz		1 tbsp		$8.75/9 lb	100		
12. Celery seed 1 cup = 4 oz		1 tsp		$5.29/lb	100		
					TOTAL RECIPE COST		

FOOD COST FORM 3

Menu Item: Wilted Spinach Salad   Date:

Number of Portions: 8   Size:

Cost per Portion: Selling Price: Food Cost %: 30%

Ingredients	Recipe Quantity (EP)			Cost			Total Cost
	Weight	Volume	Count	APC/Unit	Yield %	EPC/Unit	
1. Bacon	8 oz			$2.61/lb	100		
2. Shallots, minced 1 tbsp = 0.4 oz		4 tbsp		$1.01/lb	80		
3. Garlic, minced 1 cup = 4.6 oz		2 tsp		$1.72/lb	87		
4. Brown sugar 1 cup = 8 oz		½ cup		$0.66/lb	100		
5. Cider vinegar		⅓ cup		$4.39/gal	100		
6. Vegetable oil		6 fl oz		$6.06/5 qt	100		
7. Salt 1 cup = 10.5 oz		2 tsp		$0.38/ 1 lb 10 oz	100		
8. Pepper 1 tbsp = 0.25 oz		1 tsp		$4.99/lb	100		
9. Spinach	1½ lb			$0.77/lb	70		
10. Eggs, hard-cooked			5 ea	$0.62/doz	100		
11. Mushrooms	6 oz			$4.95/3 lb	95		
12. Red onion	3 oz			$0.40/lb	85		
13. Croutons 1 cup = 3 oz		1½ cups		$1.69/lb	100		
						TOTAL RECIPE COST	

FOOD COST FORM 4

Menu Item: Grilled Soft-Shell Crabs   Date:

Number of Portions: 10 servings   Size:

Cost per Portion: Selling Price: Food Cost %: 34%

| Ingredients | Recipe Quantity (EP) | | | Cost | | | Total |
	Weight	Volume	Count	APC/Unit	Yield %	EPC/Unit	Cost
1. Red wine vinegar		14 fl oz		$1.07/L	100		
2. Dry white wine		14 fl oz		$4.02/1.5 L	100		
3. Olive oil, extra virgin		3 fl oz		$4.42/ 750 mL	100		
4. Red pepper, minced	2 oz			$2.99/lb	84		
5. Scallions, minced (1 cup = 2 oz) (1 bunch = 3.5 oz)	2 oz			$0.26/ bunch	82		
6. Jalapeños, peeled, seeded, chopped	1 oz			$1.59/lb	81		
7. Garlic, minced (1 cup = 4.6 oz)		2 tbsp		$1.73/lb	87		
8. Basil, chopped (1 bunch = 2.5 oz) (1 tbsp = 0.088 oz)		1 tbsp		$0.56/ bunch	56		
9. Fennel tops, chopped (1 cup = 3 oz)		1 tbsp		$0.98/lb	92		
10. Tarragon, chopped (1 bunch = 1 oz) (1 tbsp = 0.114 oz)		1 tbsp		$0.48/ bunch	80		
11. Thyme, chopped (1 bunch = 1 oz) (1 tbsp = 0.1 oz)		1 tbsp		$0.46/ bunch	65		
12. Soft-shell crabs, large, cleaned			10 ea	$3.28/ea	100		
						TOTAL RECIPE COST	

FOOD COST FORM 5

Using the following information and the blank food cost form, find the cost per portion and selling price based on a projected food cost percent of 20 percent. Not all of the information given in this problem is required to solve the problem.

Angel Food Cake with Tropical Fruit Compote

The Recipe Yields Five 20-cm Cakes—6 Servings Each with Compote

1.	Sugar	900 g
2.	Cake flour	370 g
3.	Salt	8 g
4.	Egg white	900 g
5.	Cream of tartar	8 g
6.	Vanilla	5 mL
7.	Pineapple, fresh, cleaned and cubed	890 g
8.	Banana, peeled, sliced	530 g
9.	Kiwi, peeled, sliced	600 g
10.	Lime juice	150 mL
11.	Mango, peeled, sliced	750 g
12.	Coconut, fresh, grated	100 g

As-Purchased Costs

1.	Sugar	$17.99/50 lb
2.	Cake flour	$9.20/50 lb
3.	Salt	$0.38/1 lb 10 oz
4.	Egg white	$0.94/doz
5.	Cream of tartar	$12.97/12 lb jar
6.	Vanilla	$22.80/qt
7.	Pineapple	$3.64/ea
8.	Banana	$0.42/lb
9.	Kiwi	$0.29/ea
10.	Lime juice	$0.19/ea
11.	Mango	$1.49/ea
12.	Coconut	$0.60/ea

Volume to Weight Conversions and Yield Percents

1.	Sugar	1 cup = 8 oz		
2.	Cake flour	1 cup = 3 1/3 oz		
3.	Salt	1 cup = 10.5 oz		
4.	Egg white	1 egg yields 1.2 oz of egg white. Ignore the cost of the yolk.		
5.	Cream of tartar	1 cup = 4.7 oz		
6.	Vanilla	1 cup = 8 fl oz		
7.	Pineapple, fresh, cleaned and cubed	1 ea = 4 lb AP	1 cup = 6 oz	Y% = 52%
8.	Banana		1 cup = 5 oz	Y% = 68%
9.	Kiwi	1 ea = 5 oz AP	1 cup = 6 oz	Y% = 68%
10.	Lime juice	1 ea = 2.2 oz	1 cup = 8 oz	Y% = 35%
11.	Mango	1 ea = 14 oz AP	1 cup = 7.5 oz	Y% = 68%
12.	Coconut	1 ea = 26 oz AP	1 cup = 2.5 oz	Y% = 53%

172

FOOD COST FORM 5

Menu Item: Date:

Number of Portions: Size:

Cost per Portion: Selling Price: Food Cost %:

Ingredients	Recipe Quantity (EP)			Cost			Total Cost
	Weight	Volume	Count	APC/Unit	Yield %	EPC/Unit	
						TOTAL RECIPE COST	

Complete the following food cost form:

FOOD COST FORM 6

Menu Item: Red Snapper with Tropical Tubers   Date:

Number of Portions: 30 servings   Size:

Cost per Portion: Selling Price: Food Cost %: 30%

| Ingredients | Recipe Quantity (EP) | | | Cost | | | Total |
	Weight	Volume	Count	APC/Unit	Yield %	EPC/Unit	Cost
1. Red snapper	11 lb 3 oz			$8.91/lb	100		
2. Key lime juice (1 ea = 1 oz)		¾ cup		$1.39/lb	42		
3. Onions (1 cup = 0.66 lb)	3 lb 14 oz			$0.35/lb	89		
4. Yams	4 lb			$0.99/lb	79		
5. Cumin (1 tbsp = 0.016 lb) (1 jar = 12 oz)		½ cup		$12.95/jar	100		
6. Olive oil (1 bottle = 1.5 L)		1½ cups		$7.99/ bottle	100		
7. Fresh oregano (1 cup = 0.20 lb) (1 bunch = 4.5 oz)		¾ cup		$1.99/ bunch	62		
8. Garlic (1 bulb = 2 oz)	7½ oz			$0.99/bulb	89		
9. Yucca (1 cup = 7 oz)		6 cups		$0.69/lb	90		
10. Bell peppers	1 lb 12 oz			$1.29/lb	89		
11. Jalapeños (1 ea = 1 oz)	15 oz			$2.99/lb	60		
12. Salt (1 cup = 10⅔ oz)		2½ tsp		$0.39/3 lb	100		
						TOTAL RECIPE COST	

13. How many pounds of yucca should you order to make the Red Snapper with Tropical Tubers?

_____

_____

_____

_____

_____

Yield Percent: When to Ignore It

Y ou will be making pear sorbet for a party that you are catering on the last Saturday of the month. The next day, you will be making poached pears, and you would like to order the pears for these two events in advance.

The pear sorbet requires 15.75 pounds of peeled, cored, and diced pears for the 84 guests to be served. To determine the amount that needs to be ordered, divide the edible portion quantity by the yield percent, as discussed in Chapter 8, page 108. From the Approximate Yield of Fruits and Vegetables Chart, page 95, you know that the yield percent for pears is 76 percent. So

15.75 pounds ÷ 0.76 = 20.72, or 21 pounds

You should order 21 pounds of pears for this recipe.

For poached pears 36 pears are required for the 36 portions. An average pear weighs 7 ounces, as purchased. Multiply to calculate the number of pounds of pears needed to equal 36 pears: 36×7 ounces = 252 ounces, or 15.75 pounds of pears. How many pounds of pears will have to be ordered for this event? Would yield percent be used in this situation? No, it is not necessary to use yield percent to calculate quantity in this instance. In this chapter, we investigate why.

- Identify the circumstances when the yield percent does not need to be taken into account when calculating the as-purchased quantity.

- Identify the circumstances when the yield percent does not need to be taken into account when calculating the edible portion cost.

- Apply the costing principles to calculate the Total Cost and Cost per Portion in the Excel food cost form that can be found at http://www.wiley.com/go/culinarymath.

WHEN TO USE YIELD PERCENT

When is the yield percent used to calculate the amount to order?

For the sorbet mentioned in the introduction to the chapter, 15.75 pounds of cleaned pears are needed. Unless pears are being bought cleaned and trimmed, waste must be accounted for by dividing the edible portion quantity by the yield percent (see Chapter 8, page 108) because the pears must be fabricated before they are used.

In a recipe such as that for poached pears, 36 pears are needed to serve 36 people. Should yield percent be used in this case? No, because the recipe calls for 1 pear per portion. You may still trim and clean the pears, but it will not be necessary to order more pears to make up the trim loss.

If a recipe lists an ingredient that has less than 100 percent yield by count, it is most likely not necessary to use the yield percent. For example, if a recipe calls for 3 cloves of garlic, it is not necessary to have more than 3 cloves to account for waste, even though garlic does not have a 100 percent yield. In this recipe the garlic is called for in the as-purchased quantity; therefore, yield percent should not be taken into account. (See page 110 for exceptions.)

The photograph above captures the process necessary to make pears into pear sorbet. On the left, you see the pears that you purchased (APQ). In the center, the plate holds the peeled, diced pears (EPQ) with the peels (trim) off to the side. The end result, pear sorbet, is in the bowl on the far right.

177

The photograph above captures the process of preparing poached pears. On the left you see the pears that you purchased (APQ). In the center are the peeled pears (EPQ) and the peels (trim). The end result, the poached pears, are on the plate on the far right. Even though the pears are trimmed for the poached pears, the yield percent need not be taken into account because each serving is one pear. The loss of the peels does not affect the amount to order. On the other hand, the weight of the pears that are ordered for the sorbet is directly affected by the trimming of the peels. Therefore, the yield percent needs to be used when calculating the amount to order so that you have enough peeled and diced pears for the sorbet.

WHAT HAPPENS TO COST?

The way cost is calculated is affected when calculating the as-purchased quantity for a recipe that calls for ingredients by the piece or each. In Chapter 10, page 141, the as-purchased cost was changed to the edible portion cost to take trim loss into account. When costing a recipe that calls for ingredients by the piece or each (ingredients placed in the count column on a food cost form), that amount is actually, with a few exceptions (on the next page), the as-purchased quantity. Therefore, there is no need to use the yield percent to calculate the edible portion cost because it is not necessary to buy more product to compensate for the trim loss.

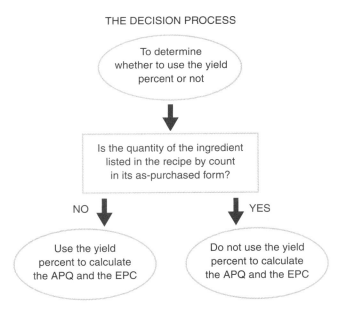

THE DECISION PROCESS

To determine whether to use the yield percent or not

Is the quantity of the ingredient listed in the recipe by count in its as-purchased form?

NO — Use the yield percent to calculate the APQ and the EPC

YES — Do not use the yield percent to calculate the APQ and the EPC

Let's apply this information to food costing. Using the pear examples, we will cost out the pears for each recipe.

Ingredients	Recipe Quantity (EP)			Cost			Total Cost
	Weight	Volume	Count	APC/Unit	Yield %	EPC/Unit	
Pears (for sorbet)	15.75 lb			$0.75/lb	76		
				0.75 ÷ 0.76 = $0.9868/lb			
					15.75 lb × $0.9868/lb = $15.55		$15.55
Pears (for poached pears) (1 ea = 7 oz)			36 ea	$0.75/lb	76	$0.75/lb	
			36 ea × 7 oz = 252	*oz ÷ 16 oz = 15.75 lb*			
					15.75 lb × $0.75 = $11.82		$11.82

Notice that even though the weight of the pears is the same in both recipes, the cost is different. The main difference is that the weight of the pears for the sorbet is an edible portion quantity and the weight of the pears for the poached pears is an as-purchased quantity; the math must be different to reflect this difference.

It is important to realize that there are many different ways of writing recipes. A recipe for pear sorbet can call for 1 pound of peeled, diced pears or 3 medium pears. The final product of the recipe will be more consistent if the ingredients are listed by weight or volume because there are no absolute definitions as to what qualifies as a medium pear. Weight and volume measures are precisely defined: 1 cup of diced pears, 1 pound of peeled pears. There is no need for interpretation of the quantity.

THE EXCEPTION TO THE EXCEPTION

Some ingredients are listed in the count column on a food cost form but, nevertheless, require the use of the yield percent. This situation occurs when a recipe calls for a cut of an ingredient in its edible portion form, such as 10 melon balls, 6 tournée-cut carrots, and the like. These cuts most definitely require a yield percent because they will not be purchased prefabricated.

> **HINT**
> How an item is purchased has nothing to do with whether to use the yield percent or not. The way the item is listed in the recipe is the information that helps you determine if the yield percent should be used or not.

RECIPE COSTING USING A COMPUTER

With the increasing use of computers in the food-service industry, particularly with food costing, we are pleased to offer you an opportunity to practice recipe costing online, on an Excel food cost form. There are three practice recipes offered with the Excel form. To access the Excel food cost form, recipes, and directions, see http://www.wiley.com/go/culinarymath.

179

CHAPTER REVIEW

Knowing the instances when yield percent is not necessary in calculating the edible portion quantity, the as-purchased quantity, and the edible portion cost is vital. Keep in mind that when a recipe calls for an ingredient by the count, piece, or each, there is no need to use the yield percent to determine how much to order—you already know. However, if the recipe calls for a fabricated item, then you have to "put the trim back on" when calculating the edible portion quantity, the as-purchased quantity, or the edible portion cost by using the yield percent. It is a good idea to look over a recipe or food cost form and determine if there are any ingredients that are listed in the count column. Before you do any calculations you should determine whether the yield percent will be needed or not.

HINT
When a food cost form already has the information on it, look over the form before beginning to cost. If there are any ingredients in the count column, be careful—you might not have to use yield percent to calculate the edible portion cost.

CHAPTER PRACTICE

Answers to odd-numbered questions may be found on page 251.

1. You are making Apple Custard Tarts for a brunch for 72 people. The recipe serves 8 and requires 3 apples for each tart. Each apple weighs 7 ounces and has an 85 percent yield. How many pounds of apples will you need for this brunch?

_____

_____

_____

_____

2. You are serving pasta with broccoli for 100 people. One bunch of broccoli will serve 8 people. How many pounds of broccoli will you need to order if 1 bunch weighs 1.5 pounds and the yield for broccoli is 61 percent?

_____

_____

_____

_____

3. You will need 900 milliliters of orange juice for Citrus Tartlets. Each orange weighs approximately 6 ounces. If oranges have a 50 percent yield for juice, then how many pounds of oranges will you need for the Citrus Tartlets?

_____

_____

_____

_____

_____

4. Poached Pears with Brandy Sauce will be the dessert for tonight's buffet. If each case contains 48 pears, how many cases will be needed if each of the 300 guests will be served 1 pear for dessert and pears have a yield percent of 78 percent?

_____

_____

_____

_____

_____

5. You are making caramel apples for 12 people. If each apple weighs approximately 10 ounces and the yield percent for apples is 76 percent, how many pounds of apples do you need to order?

_____

_____

_____

_____

_____

6. You need 389 stuffed green peppers. Each green pepper weighs 7 ounces. If a case of green peppers weighs 10 kilograms, how many cases of green peppers should be ordered if the yield percent for peppers is 82 percent?

_____

_____

_____

_____

7. You are making 12 vegetarian pizzas. Each pizza contains 2 cups of chopped green pepper. Each pepper weighs 7 ounces, and 1 cup of chopped green pepper weighs 5.2 ounces. If a green pepper has a yield percent of 82 percent, how many peppers should you purchase?

_____

_____

_____

_____

_____

8. You are having a dinner party for 15 people, and one item on the menu is Avocado and Grapefruit Salad. Each salad calls for $\frac{1}{3}$ of an avocado and $\frac{1}{2}$ of a grapefruit, both peeled and seeded. How many avocados and grapefruits will you need if the yield percent for avocados is 60 percent and for grapefruit 50 percent?

_____

_____

_____

_____

_____

9. You are making Strawberry Napoleons for a party with 16 guests. The recipe calls for 50 strawberries. The yield percent for large strawberries is 87 percent. We purchase strawberries by the pint, and each pint contains 13 berries and weighs approximately 11 ounces. Strawberries cost $1.75 per pint. How many pints of strawberries should we purchase, and how much will each serving cost?

_____

_____

_____

_____

_____

Complete the following chart:

The Situation	Use the Yield Percent?	Why or Why Not?
10. A recipe calls for 6 cups of diced pears.		
11. A recipe calls for 3 grapefruits, juiced.		
12. A recipe calls for 2 tablespoons of chopped garlic, but you are buying garlic by the bulb.		
13. The recipe calls for 1 bunch of parsley, chopped.		

FOOD COST FORM 14

Menu Item: Chayote Salad with
            Oranges   Date:

Number of Portions: 10   Size:

Cost per Portion: Selling Price: Food Cost %: 25%

Ingredients	Recipe Quantity (EP)			Cost			Total Cost
	Weight	Volume	Count	APC/Unit	Yield %	EPC/Unit	
A. Chayotes, julienne 1 ea = 7 oz			3 ea	$0.69/ea	85		
B. Jicoma, julienne	8 oz			$0.74/lb	81		
C. Carrots, julienne	8 oz			$0.35/lb	82		
D. Oranges, sections 1 ea = 8.5 oz			5 ea	$0.20/ea	35		
E. Green onions 1 bunch = 0.33 lb			1½ bunch	$0.32/ bunch	60		
F. Lime juice 1 ea = 2.2 oz		90 mL		$0.28/ea	35		
G. Sugar 1 cup = 8 oz		1½ tsp		$22.40/ 50 lb			
H. Salt 1 tbsp = $\frac{2}{3}$ oz		1 tsp		$1.62/26 oz			
I. Pepper, ground 1 tbsp = 0.25 oz		½ tsp		$6.12/lb			
J. Olive oil		3 fl oz		$24.84/gal			
K. Cilantro 1 bunch = 2.8 oz 1 cup = 1.37 oz		1 tbsp		$0.37/ bunch	46		
L. Mint 1 bunch = 3.35 oz 1 cup = 1.6 oz		1 tsp		$0.48/ bunch	41		
						TOTAL RECIPE COST	

FOOD COST FORM 15

Menu Item: Eastern Mediterranean
Bread Salad   Date:

Number of Portions: 10   Size:

Cost per Portion: Selling Price: Food Cost %: 30%

Ingredients	Recipe Quantity (EP)			Cost			Total
	Weight	Volume	Count	APC/Unit	Yield %	EPC/Unit	Cost
A. Pita bread	2 lb			$1.99/lb			
B. Olive oil		540 mL		$24.84/gal			
C. Red wine vinegar		5 fl oz		$5.87/gal			
D. Garlic, minced 1 cup = 4.6 oz		1 tbsp		$2.50/lb	87		
E. Thyme, chopped 1 tbsp = 0.1 oz 1 bunch = 1 oz	½ oz			$0.32/ bunch	60		
F. Cayenne pepper 1 tbsp = 0.2 oz		½ tsp		$5.06/ 12 oz			
G. Sugar 1 cup = 8 oz		1 tbsp		$22.40/ 50 lb			
H. Salt 1 tbsp = ⅔ oz		2 tsp		$1.62/ 26 oz			
I. Pepper, ground 1 tbsp = 0.25 oz		1 tsp		$6.12/lb			
J. Green onions 1 bunch = 0.33 lb			2 bunches	$0.32/ bunch	60		
K. Parsley 1 bunch = 3.4 oz			1 bunch	$0.46/ bunch	52		
L. Plum tomatoes, chopped	2 lb			$0.48/lb	93		
M. Cucumbers 1 ea = 12 oz			4 ea	$0.93/ea	95		
N. Radishes 1 bag = 4 oz	10 oz			$0.32/bag	92		
O. Yellow pepper 1 ea = 10 oz			1 ea	$2.13/lb	84		
					TOTAL RECIPE COST		

Beverage Costing

Your restaurant is featuring a drink special this evening:

Pear Martinis

  750 mL premium vodka
  12 fl oz clear pear brandy
  6 fl oz simple syrup
  3 limes, juiced
  3 pears, quartered

The recipe makes approximately twelve 4-fluid ounce servings. You need to determine the cost of making this drink so that you can calculate the appropriate selling price.

Similar to the costing of food, the costing of beverages is an important part of food-service cost control. Most establishments separate food cost from beverage cost. In fact, if you look at the profit-and-loss statement of a restaurant, you will see food cost and beverage cost as separate items.

In this chapter, we will look at beverage costing. As you work through this chapter you will notice that most of the principles covered in Chapter 11, "Recipe Costing," and Chapter 12, "Yield Percent: When to Ignore It," apply to beverage costing. In addition, you will be tapping into the math of Chapter 3, "Metric Measures." Since wines and spirits are purchased in liters and served in fluid ounces, it will become necessary to convert.

- Calculate the number of U.S. standard-measure servings of wine or spirits that can be poured from a quantity given in metric measure.

- Calculate the beverage cost percent given the cost per beverage and the selling price.

- Calculate the selling price for a beverage given the beverage cost percent and the cost per beverage.

BEVERAGE COST PERCENT

The beverage cost percent is similar to the food cost percent, which was discussed in Chapter 11, page 154. Food cost percent and beverage cost percent are the percent of the selling price that pays for the food or beverage. When the food cost percent is 30 percent, the amount of the selling price that goes for food cost is 30 percent. When the beverage cost percent is 14 percent, the amount of the selling price for a drink that pays for the beverage is 14 percent.

> **HINT**
> It is very important to make sure that the units are the same for the cost and the sales before you divide.

$$\text{Beverage cost percent} = \frac{\text{Beverage cost}}{\text{Beverage sales}}$$

EXAMPLE 1:

A case of liter bottles of vodka costs $180.95. The case should generate $1,389.62 in sales. What is the beverage cost percent?

$$\text{Beverage cost percent} = \frac{\text{Beverage cost}}{\text{Beverage sales}} = \frac{\$180.95}{\$1,389.62} = 13.02\%$$

EXAMPLE 2:

A liter bottle of premium gin costs $24.78. How many $1\frac{1}{2}$-ounce drinks can be poured from the bottle? If $7.50 is charged for the $1\frac{1}{2}$-ounce drink, what is the beverage cost percent?

$$\frac{33.8 \ \text{fl oz}}{1} \times \frac{1 \ \text{drink}}{1\frac{1}{2} \ \text{fl oz}} = \frac{33.8}{1.5} = 22.53333, \text{ or } 22 \text{ drinks}$$

22 drinks $\times$ $7.50 per drink = $165.00

$$\text{Beverage cost percent} = \frac{\text{Beverage cost}}{\text{Beverage sales}} = \frac{\$24.78}{\$165.00} = 15.01\%$$

187

DETERMINING COST PER BEVERAGE

Once you have calculated how much a beverage costs to make, the cost per portion can be calculated with the following formula:

$$\text{Cost per beverage} = \frac{\text{Total beverage cost}}{\text{Number of servings}}$$

EXAMPLE 1:

The wine special tonight is a Cabernet Sauvignon, which you purchase in 750-mL bottles for $15.45 per bottle. Each bottle will serve five people. How much does each serving cost?

$$\text{Cost per beverage} = \frac{\$15.45}{5 \text{ servings}} = \$3.09 \text{ per serving}$$

DETERMINING BEVERAGE SELLING PRICE USING THE BEVERAGE COST PERCENT

The cost per beverage is used to calculate the selling price based on a desired beverage cost percent.

$$\text{Selling price} = \frac{\text{Cost per beverage}}{\text{Beverage cost percent (in decimal form)}}$$

EXAMPLE 2:

Using the information from the above example, determine the selling price for one serving of Cabernet Sauvignon if the beverage cost percent is 25 percent.

$$\text{Selling price} = \frac{\$3.09}{0.25} = \$12.36$$

The price calculated using a beverage cost percent is the lowest price you can charge and maintain that beverage cost percent. Many establishments will then adjust the selling price to a more reasonable menu price. In this example, $12.36 would probably be adjusted to $12.50.

Often, the selling price is based on the total beverage cost. For instance, you are catering a party and you need the selling price for iced tea for all of the guests. In this case, you would use the following formula:

188

$$\text{Selling price} = \frac{\text{Total beverage cost}}{\text{Beverage cost percent (in decimal form)}}$$

There are many different ways to calculate the selling price for a beverage item. The method addressed in this textbook is related to the mathematical formulas above. Other resources approach selling price differently. These different methods should be researched before choosing beverage prices.

THE COST PER BEVERAGE, SELLING PRICE, AND BEVERAGE COST PERCENT TRIANGLE

The following triangle is a tool used to find the cost per beverage, selling price, and beverage cost percent. It is identical to the percent triangle introduced in Chapter 1, page 12, although the application differs.

PART = Cost per beverage

WHOLE = Selling price

PERCENT = Beverage cost percent

STEPS FOR USING THE BEVERAGE COST PERCENT TRIANGLE

STEP 1. Determine what you are looking for: cost per beverage, selling price, or beverage cost percent.

STEP 2. *To find the cost per beverage*
Cover the cost per beverage in the triangle.

Selling price and beverage cost percent are side by side. This directs you to multiply the selling price by the beverage cost percent. (Remember to change the percent to a decimal by dividing by 100 before multiplying.)

To find the selling price
Cover the selling price in the triangle.

Cost per beverage is over beverage cost percent. This directs you to divide the cost per beverage by the beverage cost percent. (Remember to change the percent to a decimal by dividing by 100 before multiplying.)

To find the beverage cost percent
Cover the beverage cost percent in the triangle.

Cost per beverage is over selling price. This directs you to divide the cost per beverage by the selling price and multiply the answer by 100 to convert it to the beverage cost percent.

189

APPLYING THE BEVERAGE COST FORMULAS

In the previous chapters, a food cost form was used to determine the cost of the food in a recipe. This form facilitates determining edible portion cost. In determining beverage cost, the yield percent for *most* beverages is 100 percent. Therefore, using a food cost form to determine the cost of beverages is optional. Once you determine the beverage cost percent, you can use it to calculate the selling price.

In the beginning of this chapter, the following problem was introduced. In order to solve this problem, you will need more information. Since fruit is being used, you must decide if yield percent should be applied. As mentioned in the previous chapter, when fruit is listed in a recipe by the piece or each, it is not necessary to apply the yield percent when costing. We will, however, need pricing information, which is given in the table below. When you are working in the food-service industry, you will need to refer to invoices to obtain this information.

EXAMPLE 1:

Your restaurant is having a drink special this evening. You will be offering Pear Martinis. The ingredients for Pear Martinis is as follows:

> 750 mL premium vodka
> 12 fl oz clear pear brandy
> 6 fl oz simple syrup
> 3 limes, juiced
> 3 pears, quartered

The recipe makes approximately twelve 4-fl-oz servings. Determine the cost per drink so that you can calculate the appropriate selling price if the desired beverage cost percent is 18 percent. The solution is found by using the following information and formulas:

Ingredients	Cost Information
1. 750 mL premium vodka	$281.16/12 L
2. 12 fl oz clear pear brandy	$19.23/750 mL
3. 6 fl oz simple syrup	$0.82/qt
4. 3 limes, juiced	$0.28/ea
5. 3 pears, quartered	$0.31/ea

STEP 1. Calculate total beverage cost.

1. Vodka

$$\frac{\$281.16}{12\ L} = \$23.43 \text{ per L}$$

$$\$23.43 \text{ per L} \times 0.75\ L = \$17.5725 = \$17.58$$

2. Clear pear brandy

$$\frac{750 \; \cancel{mL}}{1} \times \frac{33.8 \; \text{fl oz}}{1000 \; \cancel{mL}} = 25.35 \; \text{fl oz}$$

$$\frac{\$19.23}{25.35 \; \text{fl oz}} = \$0.7585 \; \text{per fl oz}$$

$$12 \; \text{fl oz} \times \$0.7585 \; \text{per fl oz} = \$9.1029 = \$9.11$$

3. Simple syrup

$$\frac{\$0.82}{32 \; \text{fl oz}} = \$0.0256 \; \text{per fl oz}$$

$$6 \; \text{fl oz} \times \$0.0256 \; \text{per fl oz} = \$0.1536 = \$0.16$$

4. Limes

$$1 \; \text{lime} = \$0.28$$

$$3 \; \text{limes} \times \$0.28 = \$0.84$$

5. Pears

$$1 \; \text{pear} = \$0.31$$

$$3 \; \text{pears} \times \$0.31 = \$0.93$$

Ingredients	Total Ingredient Cost
1. 750 mL premium vodka	$17.58
2. 12 fl oz clear pear brandy	$9.11
3. 6 fl oz simple syrup	$0.16
4. 3 limes	$0.84
5. 3 pears	$0.93
Total beverage cost:	28.62

STEP 2. Calculate the cost per beverage.

The total beverage cost is $28.62, and it makes 12 servings.

$$\text{Cost per beverage} = \frac{\text{Total beverage cost}}{\text{Number of servings}}$$

$$= \frac{\$28.62}{12 \; \text{servings}} = \$2.385 \; \text{per serving}$$

STEP 3. Calculate the selling price.

$$\text{Selling price} = \frac{\text{Cost per beverage}}{\text{Beverage cost percent (in decimal form)}}$$

$$= \frac{\$2.385 \; \text{per serving}}{0.18} = \$13.25 \; \text{for 1 pear martini}$$

You are catering a wedding brunch for 230 guests. You predict that each guest will have approximately 2 cups of coffee. A pound of coffee will make 50 cups. The bride has requested a special blend of coffee, Kenya AA, a high-quality coffee from Africa. This coffee can be purchased for $7.95 a pound. You need to estimate the cost of the coffee for this brunch in order to determine the selling price if the desired beverage cost percent is 30 percent.

STEP 1. Calculate the total beverage cost.
We are costing 2 cups of coffee for 230 guests.

$$230 \times 2 \text{ cups} = 460 \text{ cups total}$$

$$\frac{460 \text{ cups}}{1} \times \frac{1 \text{ lb}}{50 \text{ cups}} = \frac{460}{50} = 9.2 \text{ lb of coffee needed to make 460 cups}$$

$$\text{Total cost} = \text{Number of units} \times \text{Cost per unit} = 9.2 \text{ lb} \times \$7.95 \text{ per lb} = \$73.14$$

The total beverage cost is $73.14

STEP 2. Calculate the selling price.

$$\text{Selling price} = \frac{\text{Total beverage cost}}{\text{Beverage cost percent (in decimal form)}}$$

$$= \frac{\$73.14}{0.30} = \$243.80 \text{ for the coffee for this wedding brunch}$$

CHAPTER REVIEW

The sale of beverages in a food-service establishment can potentially be very profitable. It is essential that management maintain control over this area to ensure these profits are realized.

$$\text{Beverage cost percent} = \frac{\text{Beverage cost}}{\text{Beverage sales}}$$

$$\text{Cost per beverage} = \frac{\text{Total beverage cost}}{\text{Number of servings}}$$

$$\text{Selling price} = \frac{\text{Cost per beverage}}{\text{Beverage cost percent (in decimal form)}}$$

BEVERAGE COST PERCENT TRIANGLE

PART = Cost per beverage

WHOLE = Selling price

PERCENT = Beverage cost percent

CHAPTER PRACTICE

Answers to odd-numbered questions may be found on page 251.

1. You are catering a wedding for 350 people. You predict that each guest will have two 5-ounce glasses of wine. The wine is purchased at $90.00 per case, 9 liters per case.

A. How many cases will you need?

_____

_____

_____

_____

_____

B. How much will it cost per guest?

_____

_____

_____

_____

_____

2. A restaurant orders 5 cases (750-milliliter bottles) of red wine in the beginning of the week. There are 12 bottles in a case. They pay $297 for the 5 cases. At the end of the week there are 18 bottles left. Answer the following questions:

A. What percent of the cases were sold?

_____

_____

_____

_____

_____

B. If each bottle sold for $21.50, what is the beverage cost percent?

_____

_____

_____

_____

_____

c. If we decided to sell the remaining bottles by the glass, how many glasses could be poured if each glass held 6 ounces?

_____

_____

_____

_____

_____

3. The beverage cost percent is 16.5 percent for 750-milliliter bottles of imported water. If you purchase a 10-case lot for $122 and there are 12 bottles in a case, then:

A. What is the cost per bottle?

_____

_____

_____

_____

_____

B. How much should you charge for each bottle?

_____

_____

_____

_____

_____

4. You charge $5.50 for a 3 1/2-ounce portion of wine. Your beverage cost percent is 15 percent.

    A. What is the beverage cost of one serving of wine?

_____

_____

_____

_____

_____

    B. The bartender accidentally starts pouring 5-ounce glasses of wine. If the selling price remains the same, what will be the new beverage cost percent?

_____

_____

_____

_____

    C. What will happen to profits if this is not corrected?

_____

_____

_____

_____

5. Your restaurant is hosting a New Year's Eve party for 225 people. Each person is to receive two 2.5-ounce glasses of complimentary champagne. You will also need 2 bottles of champagne to give away as door prizes. How many cases must you buy if you purchase 750-milliliter bottles that are packed 12 to a case?

_____

_____

_____

_____

6. You will be serving approximately 20 guests a 4-ounce glass of Pinot Grigio. How many 750-milliliter bottles should you order?

_____

_____

_____

_____

_____

7. If you purchase a liter bottle of whiskey, how many 1 ¼-ounce drinks can be poured from one bottle?

_____

_____

_____

_____

_____

8. The house purchases 3 cases of gin in liter bottles, 12 per case, for $575.28. If the house pours 1 ¾-ounce drinks, how many drinks can be poured from the 3 cases? How much will each drink cost?

_____

_____

_____

_____

_____

9. A measured liter bottle of vodka has 350 milliliters remaining. What percent of the bottle has been poured? If the bottle cost is $23.43, then what is the value of the amount of vodka that remains?

_____

_____

_____

_____

_____

10. A case of 750-milliliter bottles of tequila costs $178.50 and contains 12 bottles. If this same tequila can be purchased in liter-size bottles, 12 in a case, the case would cost $228.00. Explain which case is the better buy.

_____

_____

_____

_____

_____

11. The beverage cost percent on a $1\frac{3}{4}$-ounce drink of spirits is 12 percent. The drink costs you $0.82. How much are you charging for the drink?

_____

_____

_____

_____

_____

12. You purchase 5 cases of Chardonnay. Each case contains twelve 750-milliliter bottles. Each case costs $98.40. You are planning to sell the wine in 6-ounce glasses for $6.25. What is the beverage cost percent?

_____

_____

_____

_____

_____

13. Three cases of liter-size bottles (12 per case) of vodka are purchased for $850. If the bartender pours $1\frac{1}{4}$-ounce drinks, how many drinks can be poured from the 3 cases? If each drink sells for $5.95, what is the beverage cost percent?

_____

_____

_____

_____

_____

14. You receive a case of rum that contains twelve 750-milliliter bottles. The case cost $160. You will be serving the rum in 1 ³/₄-ounce servings. How many servings can be obtained from this case?

_____

_____

_____

_____

_____

15. How many full servings can be poured from a case of 1.5-liter bottles (6 per case) if each glass of wine will contain 4 ounces?

_____

_____

_____

_____

_____

16. A liter bottle of rum costs $18.75. If 40 percent of the bottle remains, then what is the value of the amount used?

_____

_____

_____

_____

_____

17. You are making a special chocolate drink for 45 guests. Each drink requires 1 ¹/₂ ounces of chocolate liquor, which is purchased in 750-milliliter bottles. How many bottles of chocolate liquor should you order?

_____

_____

_____

_____

_____

18. You sell glasses of freshly squeezed lemonade for $4.75. If you use a 20 percent beverage cost, then what is your cost for the glass of lemonade?

_____

_____

_____

_____

_____

Recipe Size Conversion

Y ou are a private chef and must accommodate many parties of varying sizes. Next week there are two dinner parties scheduled. The first dinner is for 6 people. The hostess wants to serve Chicken in Phyllo Dough, but this recipe yields 20 portions. For the other dinner scheduled, she has requested Lobster Bisque. Your recipe yields 1 gallon, but for this dinner you will need ten 5-ounce portions. Converting recipe yields can become tricky. However, you can follow the steps covered in this chapter to simplify the process while still maintaining the integrity of the original recipe.

Converting recipes is one of the most important skills that you will need in the food-service industry. It allows you to produce the proper amount of almost any given recipe. This flexibility will help you to control food cost by ensuring that the recipe is not overproduced, which creates additional food waste and therefore higher food cost. Additionally, the ability to convert a recipe to produce a larger quantity prevents underproduction, thereby avoiding unhappy and dissatisfied customers.

OBJECTIVES

- Calculate a recipe conversion factor to make a desired quantity of a given recipe.

- Compute the new ingredient quantities using the recipe conversion factor.

- Convert difficult-to-measure quantities into easier-to-measure quantities.

USING THE RECIPE CONVERSION FACTOR TO CONVERT RECIPE YIELDS

Recipes produce a specific yield in the form of weight, volume, or count. For example, a recipe can yield 3 pounds of pie dough, 2 gallons of vinaigrette, or 12 servings of Peach Melba. Often it is necessary to alter the yield of a recipe to accommodate particular needs. To convert the yield of a recipe, several steps should be followed to ensure that the product will have the same taste and texture as the original recipe.

The *recipe conversion factor (RCF)* is a factor that is used to convert each recipe ingredient quantity so that the new recipe yields the new desired amount. The RCF is calculated by dividing the new desired recipe yield by the old or original recipe yield. The decimal answer is the recipe conversion factor. The most critical part of this calculation is making sure that the units for the new recipe and the old recipe are the same before you divide. Once calculated correctly, this factor may be used to adjust the ingredient quantities in the original recipe to fit the desired yield.

NOTE

Keep in mind that the term *yield* has more than one meaning in the culinary world. In this chapter, the term *yield* refers to the total quantity that a recipe produces. In Chapter 7, *yield percent* referred to the percent of an ingredient that is edible.

CALCULATING THE RECIPE CONVERSION FACTOR

A recipe conversion factor (RCF) represents the relationship between the **New** and **Old** recipe yields. There are three **NO**s in calculating RCF:

1. $\dfrac{\text{New recipe yield}}{\text{Old recipe yield}} = \dfrac{\mathbf{N}}{\mathbf{O}} = \text{Recipe Conversion Factor}$

(Be careful not to invert this—you will get **ON** instead of **NO**.)

2. **NO** rounding of the recipe conversion factor.

3. **NO** units—the recipe conversion factor carries no unit.

CALCULATING THE RECIPE CONVERSION FACTOR WITH THE SAME UNIT

Original Recipe Yield	New Recipe Yield
1. 3 pounds pie dough	20 lb pie dough
2. 2 gallons vinaigrette	½ gal vinaigrette
3. 12 servings peach melba dessert	50 servings peach melba dessert

201

1. Pie dough

$$\frac{\text{New}}{\text{Old}} = \frac{20 \ \text{lb}}{3 \ \text{lb}} = \frac{20}{3} = 6.6666 \ \text{RCF}$$

2. Vinaigrette

$$\frac{\text{New}}{\text{Old}} = \frac{0.5 \ \text{gal}}{2 \ \text{gal}} = \frac{0.5}{2} = 0.25 \ \text{RCF}$$

3. Peach Melba

$$\frac{\text{New}}{\text{Old}} = \frac{50 \ \text{servings}}{12 \ \text{servings}} = \frac{50}{12} = 4.16666 \ \text{RCF}$$

In the above examples, the new recipe yields and the old recipe yields have the same unit. This is not always the case.

CALCULATING THE RECIPE CONVERSION FACTOR WITH DIFFERENT UNITS

A recipe yields 3 quarts of soup, and the yield needs to be changed to 2 gallons. In this type of situation, in which the units are not the same, the calculations will be the same as shown, with one additional step—before you calculate the RCF, it is necessary to make sure that the unit in the old recipe match the unit in the new recipe.

$$\frac{\text{New}}{\text{Old}} = \frac{2 \ \text{gal}}{3 \ \text{qt}} = \frac{2 \ \text{gal}}{0.75 \ \text{gal}} = 2.666 \ \text{RCF}$$

$$\frac{3 \ \text{qt}}{1} \times \frac{1 \ \text{gal}}{4 \ \text{qt}} = \frac{3}{4} = 0.75 \ \text{gal}$$

Another way to find the RCF for this problem is to convert all units to quarts prior to calculating the RCF.

$$\frac{\text{New}}{\text{Old}} = \frac{2 \ \text{gal}}{3 \ \text{qt}} = \frac{8 \ \text{qt}}{3 \ \text{qt}} = 2.666 \ \text{RCF}$$

$$\frac{2 \ \text{gal}}{1} \times \frac{4 \ \text{qt}}{1 \ \text{gal}} = 8 \ \text{qt}$$

Whether all the units are converted to quarts or to gallons, the result is the same because the relationship between the two recipe yields is the same no matter what unit you convert them to. You could actually change them both to tablespoons and the RCF would be the same! However, if you converted to tablespoons, it would require more calculations and, therefore, might lead to careless mistakes.

CAUTION

Remember that changing a recipe's yield also affects the mixing time, pan size, cooking temperature, and cooking time. These cannot be adjusted by the recipe conversion factor. For instance, if you double an oatmeal raisin cookie recipe that bakes at 375°F, it would not be smart to double the temperature and bake the cookies at 750°F. As you become more familiar with the science and art of food preparation, you will learn how to handle these situations in each case.

EXAMPLES:

Original Recipe Yield	New Recipe Yield
1. 1 cup sauce	1 qt sauce
2. 1½ lb spice mix	12 oz spice mix
3. 1½ pt salsa	1¾ gal salsa

Sauce

$$\frac{\text{New}}{\text{Old}} = \frac{1 \text{ qt}}{1 \text{ cup}} = \frac{4 \text{ cups}}{1 \text{ cup}} = 4 \text{ RCF}$$

$$\frac{1 \text{ qt}}{1} \times \frac{4 \text{ cups}}{1 \text{ qt}} = 4 \text{ cups}$$

Spice Mix

$$\frac{\text{New}}{\text{Old}} = \frac{12 \text{ oz}}{1\frac{1}{2} \text{ lb}} = \frac{0.75 \text{ lb}}{1.5 \text{ lb}} = 0.5 \text{ RCF}$$

$$\frac{12 \text{ oz}}{1} \times \frac{1 \text{ lb}}{16 \text{ oz}} = \frac{12}{16} = 0.75 \text{ lb}$$

Salsa

$$\frac{\text{New}}{\text{Old}} = \frac{1\frac{3}{4} \text{ gal}}{1\frac{1}{2} \text{ pt}} = \frac{14 \text{ pt}}{1.5 \text{ pt}} = 9.333 \text{ RCF}$$

$$\frac{1.75 \text{ gal}}{1} \times \frac{8 \text{ pt}}{1 \text{ gal}} = \frac{14}{1} = 14 \text{ pt}$$

CALCULATING THE RECIPE CONVERSION FACTOR WITH PORTION SIZES

When you are using the RCF to convert portion sizes, the new and old recipe yields must first be converted to the same unit. The following example describes how to do that.

EXAMPLES:

You want to increase the yield of some family recipes for use in your restaurant. Figure the RCF using portion sizes.

Original Recipe Yield	New Recipe Yield
1. 60 5-oz portions blueberry muffins	10 dozen 4-oz blueberry muffins
2. 30 $\frac{3}{4}$-cup servings rice pudding	2 qt rice pudding
3. 48 4-oz lemon cookies	6$\frac{1}{2}$ dozen 2-oz lemon cookies

In each case, the recipe yields must be converted to the same unit before the RCF can be calculated. This may require some additional steps.

Blueberry Muffins

$$\frac{\text{New}}{\text{Old}} = \frac{120 \text{ 4-oz portions}}{60 \text{ 5-oz portions}} = \frac{120 \times 4 \text{ oz}}{60 \times 5 \text{ oz}} = \frac{480 \text{ oz}}{300 \text{ oz}} = 1.6 \text{ RCF}$$

Rice Pudding

$$\frac{\text{New}}{\text{Old}} = \frac{2 \text{ quarts}}{30 \times \frac{3}{4} \text{ cup}} = \frac{2 \text{ quarts}}{22\frac{1}{2} \text{ cups}} = \frac{8 \text{ cups}}{22\frac{1}{2} \text{ cups}} = 0.35555 \text{ RCF}$$

Lemon Cookies

$$\frac{\text{New}}{\text{Old}} = \frac{6\frac{1}{2} \text{ dozen} \times 2 \text{ oz}}{48 \times 4 \text{ oz}} = \frac{78 \times 2 \text{ oz}}{48 \times 4 \text{ oz}} = \frac{156 \text{ oz}}{192 \text{ oz}} = 0.8125 \text{ RCF}$$

As you can see from these examples, when the yield of a recipe is increased, the RCF is always greater than 1, and when the yield of a recipe is decreased, the RCF is always less than 1.

Next, we will discuss how the RCF is used to convert recipe ingredient quantities.

APPLYING THE RECIPE CONVERSION FACTOR

Red Pepper Coulis
Yield: 1 quart

> 3 pounds red peppers, chopped
> 4 ounces onion, chopped
> 2 garlic cloves, minced
> ¼ jalapeño, minced
> 2 tablespoons olive oil
> 1½ pints chicken stock
> 2 tablespoons balsamic vinegar
> ½ teaspoon salt
> Pinch black pepper

NOTE
Using the number of portions to calculate the RCF in a given problem will work only if the portion sizes are the same (both 5-ounce portions or both 8-ounce portions, for example).

Change the yield of the Red Pepper Coulis to 1½ gallons. Calculate the RCF:

$$\frac{\textbf{New}}{\textbf{Old}} = \frac{1\,\frac{1}{2}\ \text{gal}}{1\ \text{qt}} = \frac{6\ \cancel{\text{qt}}}{1\ \cancel{\text{qt}}} = 6\ \text{RCF}$$

Use the RCF, which is 6, to adjust the ingredients in the original recipe to yield the new desired amount. To accomplish this, multiply each ingredient by the RCF.

CAUTION

For most recipes, you can use the recipe conversion factor method. However, for some recipes, you need to keep in mind the following:

1. Many recipes or formulas that call for a chemical leavener such as baking powder or baking soda by volume cannot be converted using this method.

2. Be careful with spices. Many times the ingredient quantity listed in a recipe is appropriate for a range of recipe yields. As a result, you might not want to alter the amount initially. Instead you may choose to add to taste later.

3. The new recipe should always be tested in order to ensure that it has been reproduced correctly.

4. The greater the conversion of a recipe size, either up or down, the greater the chance for running into problems maintaining the integrity of the original recipe. You might find that your product is too loose, too thick, or too salty.

Be aware that RCF conversion is a mathematical way of resizing the yield on a recipe. Your knowledge of food and cooking will help you successfully resize a recipe.

RED PEPPER COULIS

Original (Old) Recipe Ingredients	RCF	New Recipe Ingredients
3 lb red peppers, chopped	× 6	18 lb
4 oz onion, chopped	× 6	24 oz
2 garlic cloves, minced	× 6	12 cloves
¼ jalapeño, minced	× 6	1½ each
2 tbsp olive oil	× 6	12 tbsp
1½ pt chicken stock	× 6	9 pt
2 tbsp balsamic vinegar	× 6	12 tbsp
½ tsp salt	× 6	3 tsp
Pinch black pepper	× 6	6 pinches black pepper

MAKING THE NEW RECIPE EASIER TO MEASURE

After calculating the RCF and the new ingredient quantities, apply your knowledge of ingredients and how they affect taste and texture, as well as your knowledge of units of measure, to adjust the new ingredient quantities to more reasonable measurements.

RED PEPPER COULIS

Original (Old) Recipe Ingredients	RCF	New Recipe Ingredients	Adjusted Ingredients
3 lb red peppers, chopped	× 6	18 lb	18 lb
For the red peppers, 18 pounds is an acceptable measurement.			
4 oz onion, chopped	× 6	24 oz	1½ lb or 1 lb 8 oz
For the onions, we could use 24 ounces or convert it to pounds.			
2 garlic cloves, minced	× 6	12 cloves	12 cloves
For the garlic cloves, 12 cloves is an acceptable measurement.			
¼ jalapeño, minced	× 6	1½ ea	1½ ea
For the jalapeño, 1½ each is fine. However, see "caution" note on page 205 for further discussion.			
2 tbsp olive oil	× 6	12 tbsp	¾ cup
For the olive oil, 12 tablespoons converts to ¾ cup.			
1½ pt chicken stock	× 6	9 pt	1 gal plus 1 pt
For the chicken stock, 9 pints is not an especially reasonable measure. Converting it to gallons makes sense.			

Original (Old) Recipe Ingredients	RCF	New Recipe Ingredients	Adjusted Ingredients
2 tbsp balsamic vinegar	× 6	12 tbsp	¾ cup

For balsamic vinegar, 12 tablespoons converts to ¾ cup.

| ½ tsp salt | × 6 | 3 tsp | 1 tbsp |

For salt, 3 tsp converts nicely to 1 tablespoon. However, see the caution on page 205 for further discussion.

| Pinch black pepper | × 6 | 6 pinches black pepper | ½ tsp |

For black pepper, a pinch is generally considered something less than ⅛ teaspoon. So, if you multiply ⅛ by 6, it becomes 6/8 or ¾ tsp. Since a pinch is less than ⅛ teaspoon, though, you should probably start with ½ teaspoon and add to taste.

Apple Cider Sauce
Yield: 1 quart

   1 quart apple cider
   3 fluid ounces cider vinegar
   1 pint fond de veau lié
   ¼ teaspoon salt
   ¼ teaspoon ground black pepper
   1½ pounds Granny Smith apples

If you would like to make just 1 cup of this sauce, you need to calculate the recipe conversion factor.

$$\frac{\textbf{New}}{\textbf{Old}} = \frac{1 \text{ cup}}{1 \text{ qt}} = \frac{1 \text{ cup}}{4 \text{ cups}} = 0.25 \text{ RCF}$$

DANGER

When changing a recipe to yield less, there is a temptation to divide. Keep in mind that you must *always* multiply by the RCF. (Multiplying by 0.25 is the same as dividing by 4.)

APPLE CIDER SAUCE

Original (Old) Recipe Ingredients	RCF	New Recipe Ingredients
1 qt apple cider	× 0.25	0.25 qt
3 fl oz cider vinegar	× 0.25	0.75 fl oz
1 pt fond de veau lié	× 0.25	0.25 pt
¼ tsp salt	× 0.25	0.0625 tsp
¼ tsp ground black pepper	× 0.25	0.0625 tsp
1½ lb Granny Smith apples	× 0.25	0.375 lb

APPLE CIDER SAUCE			
Original (Old) Recipe Ingredients	RCF	New Recipe Ingredients	Adjusted Ingredients
1 qt apple cider	× 0.25	0.25 qt	1 cup
For the apple cider, ¼ quart converts to 1 cup.			
3 fl oz cider vinegar	× 0.25	0.75 fl oz	1 tbsp plus 1¼ tsp
For the cider vinegar, converting to tablespoons makes the most sense. Since 1 tablespoon is 0.5 fluid ounce, 0.75 fluid ounce would be 1½ tablespoons. It is difficult to measure ½ tablespoon. Half of 1 tablespoon is 1½ teaspoons. So the most accurate way to measure the cider vinegar is 1 tablespoon plus 1½ teaspoons.			
1 pt fond de veau lié	× 0.25	0.25 pt	½ cup
For the fond de veau lié, ¼ pint converts to ½ cup.			
¼ tsp salt	× 0.25	0.0625 tsp	Pinch
For the salt, 0.0625 teaspoons is ¹⁄₁₆ teaspoon—too small to measure. Anything less than ⅛ (0.125 teaspoon) is a pinch.			
¼ tsp ground black pepper	× 0.25	0.0625 tsp	Pinch
For the pepper, 0.0625 teaspoons is ¹⁄₁₆ of a teaspoon—too small to measure. Anything less than ⅛ teaspoon (0.125 teaspoon) is a pinch.			
1½ lb Granny Smith apples	× 0.25	0.375 lb	6 oz
For the apples, 0.375 pound is okay, or you could change it to ounces—0.375 lb is 6 ounces.			

When adjusting the recipe at the end of this process, be careful not to alter individual amounts so much that the outcome will be affected.

HEAPING AND SCANT

Heaping describes a measure that is slightly fuller than level. For example, 1.096 tablespoon converts to a heaping tablespoon. *Scant* describes a measure that is slightly less full than level. For example, 0.98 teaspoon converts nicely to a scant teaspoon. Words such as *heaping* and *scant* might help to describe amounts that are not quite whole measures; heaping and scant measures are especially appropriate for recipes that are being developed for the home cook.

When scaling recipes up or down for use in a professional kitchen, however, and especially when creating a recipe for standard use, terms such as *heaping* and *scant* should not be used. These terms are not exact measures and cannot be used effectively for costing recipes or maintaining inventory. For this situation, the new ingredient amounts should be rounded to the nearest measurable number. If the recipe is being scaled for the creation

Scant measure, at left, does not quite fill a measuring spoon, while heaping measure, at right, slightly overfills a measuring spoon.

of a standard recipe, the newly calculated recipe should be tested and any necessary alterations made.

It is important to remember that you should always go back to the original recipe to convert a recipe again. For instance, if you wanted to make 1 gallon of the apple cider sauce, you should convert from the original recipe, not from the adjusted recipe.

Bakers' percent calculates the weight of all ingredients in a bread recipe based on a percent of the total weight of the flour.

THE BAKERS' PERCENT

In baking and pastry, there is an additional method used to adjust recipes, which is called the *bakers' percent*. The values of bakers' percents are derived from an existing formula or recipe, which has flour as an ingredient. Flour is assigned the value of 100 percent (the whole), and the other ingredient values are calculated based on the flour.

EXAMPLE:

STEPS FOR CALCULATING BAKERS' PERCENT

STEP 1. Convert all ingredient quantities to the same unit.

STEP 2. Using the quantity of the flour as 100 percent (the whole), determine the percents of the remaining ingredients.

Convert the following recipe for Basic Lean Dough to a bakers' percent for Basic Lean Dough.

Basic Lean Dough Recipe

3 pounds water
⅓ ounce yeast
5 pounds bread flour
⅓ ounce salt

STEP 1. Convert all ingredient quantities to the same unit. In this problem, we will convert all the units to pounds. It would also be correct to convert all the units to ounces.

⅓ ounce of yeast

$$\frac{0.3333 \; \text{oz}}{1} \times \frac{1 \; \text{lb}}{16 \; \text{oz}} = 0.0208 \; \text{lb}$$

⅓ ounce of salt is the same as the yeast: 0.0208 pound

STEP 2. Using the quantity of the flour as 100 percent (the whole), determine the percents of the remaining ingredients.

For water:

$$\frac{3 \; \text{lbs water}}{5 \; \text{lbs bread flour}} = 0.6 \times 100 = 60\%$$

For yeast:

$$\frac{0.0208 \; \text{lb yeast}}{5 \; \text{lbs bread flour}} = 0.0041 \times 100 = 0.41\%$$

For salt:

$$\frac{0.0208 \text{ lb salt}}{5 \text{ lbs bread flour}} = 0.0041 \times 100 = 0.41\%$$

After calculating the percents, the following recipe can be represented in bakers' percents:

Basic Lean Dough Percents

60 percent water
0.41 percent yeast
100 percent bread flour
0.41 percent salt

Once you have calculated the bakers' percents you can use them to scale the formula or recipe up or down easily. For instance, suppose you want to make this bread with 25 pounds of bread flour.

Basic Lean Dough Percents	Calculation	Amount to Use
60% water	0.6 × 25 lb	15 lb
0.41% yeast	0.0041 × 25 lb	0.1025 lb or 1.64 oz
100% bread flour		25 pounds
0.41% salt	0.0041 × 25 lb	0.1025 lb or 1.64 oz

Things to remember when using bakers' percent:

- When using more than one type of flour you must add the quantities of flour together to determine 100 percent (the whole).

- Occasionally, an ingredient quantity will be greater than 100 percent if there is more of that ingredient than flour in the formula.

In addition to allowing the baker to adjust a formula (recipe), the bakers' percent allows the baker to evaluate a formula (recipe) to ensure that the formula is not defective prior to preparing the recipe.

CHAPTER REVIEW

Recipe conversion is a common occurrence in a food-service operation. Whether you are converting a recipe to give it to a customer or to serve it at a very large banquet, you will find that this approach saves time and maintains the integrity of the recipe.

The three **NO**s of calculating RCF are:

1. $\dfrac{\textbf{N}\text{ew recipe yield}}{\textbf{O}\text{ld recipe yield}} = \dfrac{\textbf{N}}{\textbf{O}} = \text{Recipe Conversion Factor}$

Be careful not to invert this—you will get **ON** instead of **NO**!

2. NO rounding of the recipe conversion factor.

3. NO units—the recipe conversion factor carries no unit.

CHAPTER PRACTICE

Answers to odd-numbered questions may be found on page 253.

1. A recipe for raspberry sauce makes 12 $\frac{1}{2}$ ounces, and the recipe calls for 7 ounces of raspberry purée. You want to make thirty 1 $\frac{1}{2}$-ounce servings. How many ounces of raspberry purée should you use?

_____

_____

_____

_____

_____

2. You have been asked to prepare Caesar Salad for 120 people. The recipe you are working with serves 8 people.

    A. What is the recipe conversion factor?

_____

_____

_____

_____

_____

    B. If the original recipe called for 1 $\frac{1}{2}$ cups of oil, how many gallons of oil should you use to make the 120 servings?

_____

_____

_____

_____

_____

3. You have a recipe for asparagus soup that yields ten 6-ounce servings of soup. The recipe calls for 1 teaspoon of lemon zest and 2 ounces of diced onions (among other ingredients).

A. You would like to use this recipe for a party you are catering for 175 guests. Each guest will receive a 5-ounce serving. How much lemon zest and diced onions should you use for the soup for this party?

_____
_____
_____
_____
_____

B. How many pounds of lemons should you order for this party if each lemon yields 2 teaspoons of zest and each lemon weighs approximately 3.5 ounces?

_____
_____
_____
_____
_____

C. How many pounds of onions should you order for this party if onions have an 87 percent yield?

_____
_____
_____
_____
_____

4. Use the following information to answer Questions 4A and 4B. Your recipe for coconut pie yields 12 pies and calls for 9 cups of shredded coconut and $1\frac{1}{2}$ cups of flour. You want to make 26 coconut pies.

A. How many cups of flour should you use?

_____
_____
_____
_____
_____

B. How many coconuts should you order?

_____

_____

_____

_____

_____

5. Use the following information to answer Questions 5A–E. A recipe for Alice's Special Chicken makes 6 servings and calls for the following ingredients:

3 each green peppers
2¼ cups chopped onion
18 ounces chicken
2 tablespoons lime juice
1½ teaspoons chili powder

A. What is the recipe conversion factor if you want to make 10 portions?

_____

_____

_____

_____

_____

B. How many pounds of chicken should you use if you make the 10 portions?

_____

_____

_____

_____

C. How many green peppers should you order if you want to make 10 portions?

_____

_____

_____

_____

D. If chili powder is purchased in 5-ounce containers for $3.99, how much will the chili powder cost for the 10 portions?

_____

_____

_____

_____

_____

E. How many pounds of onions should you order for the 10 servings?

_____

_____

_____

_____

_____

In the following problems, it is not necessary to convert the answers to more measurable units.

6. A recipe for Tuscan Fish Soup makes one hundred fifty 6-fluid-ounce servings. You will be making forty 8-fluid-ounce servings. What is the recipe conversion factor?

_____

_____

_____

_____

_____

7. A recipe for Rice Pilaf yields ten 4-ounce portions. The recipe calls for 14 ounces of long-grain white rice. How many ounces of long-grain white rice should you use if you want to make thirty 3-ounce portions of Rice Pilaf?

_____

_____

_____

_____

_____

215

8. A recipe for Spicy Moroccan Orange Salad makes 10 servings of $^3/_4$ cup each. The recipe calls for $^1/_2$ teaspoon of cayenne pepper. If you want to make 90 servings of $^1/_2$ cup each, how much cayenne pepper should you use?

_____

_____

_____

_____

_____

9. A recipe for Cream of Tomato Soup makes 3.75 liters of soup. The recipe calls for 115 grams of flour. You want to make forty 6-fluid-ounce portions of Cream of Tomato Soup. How many ounces of flour will you need to use?

_____

_____

_____

_____

_____

10. A recipe for Marinara Sauce makes 2 quarts and calls for 1 pint of tomato purée. If you need to make 100 half-cup servings, how many quarts of tomato purée should you use?

_____

_____

_____

_____

_____

11. You are making a gratin of fresh fruits. The recipe makes 8 servings. You need to make 15 servings. What is the recipe conversion factor?

_____

_____

_____

_____

_____

12. You are making Cheese-Filled Danish. A recipe for cheese filling made with baker's cheese makes $4\frac{1}{2}$ pounds of filling. The recipe calls for $2\frac{1}{2}$ pounds of cheese, $\frac{1}{4}$ fluid ounce of vanilla, and other ingredients. Each danish is to contain $1\frac{3}{4}$ ounces of the cheese filling. If you are making 25 dozen danish, how many pounds of the cheese and how many fluid ounces of the vanilla should you use?

_____

_____

_____

_____

_____

13. Explain why the recipe conversion factor is always greater than 1 when increasing a recipe and always less than 1 when decreasing a recipe.

_____

_____

_____

_____

_____

14. The following recipe for Maple Glazed Pork makes 50 servings. Adjust the recipe to make 8 servings of Maple Glazed Pork. Convert your answers to more measurable quantities.

MAPLE GLAZED PORK		
	Yield: 50 servings	Adjusted yield: 8 servings
Ingredients	Standard Quantity	Adjusted Quantity
A. Pork shoulder	18 lb	
B. Maple syrup	$1\frac{1}{2}$ qt	
C. Scallions	2 cups	
D. Orange juice	3 cups	
E. Cinnamon sticks	10 ea	
F. Nutmeg	$1\frac{1}{2}$ tsp	
G. Star anise	1 tbsp	
H. Tangerine peel	12 strips	
I. Ginger	3 tbsp	
J. Black Pepper	1 tbsp	

15. What is the major benefit to using the recipe conversion factor?

_____

_____

_____

_____

_____

16. Adjust the following recipe as indicated.

SENATE BEAN SOUP		
Ingredients	Yield: 20 servings, 6 fl oz each Standard Quantity	Adjusted yield: 60 servings, 5 fl oz each Adjusted Quantity
A. Navy beans	1½ lb	
B. Chicken stock	1 gal	
C. Ham hocks, smoked	2 each	
D. Vegetable oil	¼ cup	
E. Onions, diced	6 oz	
F. Carrots, diced	6 oz	
G. Celery, diced	6 oz	
H. Garlic clove, minced	2 each	
I. Tabasco sauce	¼ tsp	
J. Black pepper and salt	To taste	

17. A recipe for Crème Brûlée makes twenty-eight 6-ounce servings. The recipe calls for 4 quarts of heavy cream. If you want to make ninety-seven 6-ounce servings, how many gallons of heavy cream do you need?

_____

_____

_____

_____

18. You need to make spaghetti sauce for 380 people. Your current recipe calls for 20 cups of tomatoes, 4 tablespoons of chopped garlic, 1 cup of diced onions, and 1 ½ pounds of ground beef. Your recipe makes enough sauce to serve 40 people. How much of each ingredient do you need to make enough for 380 people?

_____

_____

_____

_____

_____

19. Your recipe for Barbecue Spice Mix makes 60 grams and requires ½ ounce of chili powder. If you want to make 8 ounces of your mix, then how many ounces of chili powder will you need?

_____

_____

_____

_____

_____

20. A lemonade recipe that makes eight 10-fluid-ounce servings calls for 2 cups of fresh lemon juice, 7 cups of water, and 1.5 cups of granulated sugar. You need to make one hundred 4-fluid-ounce servings for a party that you are catering. How many lemons do you need to purchase if the yield percent is 45 percent and each lemon weighs 5 ounces?

_____

_____

_____

_____

_____

21. A recipe for cheesecake makes two cakes with 16 servings each. If you want to make 80 servings, what is the recipe conversion factor?

_____

_____

_____

_____

_____

22. A recipe for margaritas calls for 10 limes for 8 servings. You will be making margaritas for 15 people. How many limes should you use?

_____

_____

_____

_____

_____

23. Name two ingredients that you have to be careful with when using the recipe conversion factor (RCF).

_____

_____

_____

_____

_____

24. A recipe for Minestrone makes 15 liters of soup and calls for 8 fluid ounces of olive oil. You would like to make twenty-four 5-fluid-ounce portions of Minestrone. How many fluid ounces of olive oil should you use?

_____

_____

_____

_____

_____

25. You are making Roasted Garlic Soup for 125 guests. Each person is to receive a 5-fluid-ounce portion of soup. You have a recipe that produces 1 ½ quarts of soup. What is the recipe conversion factor?

_____

_____

_____

_____

_____

26. A recipe for pasta makes 10 entrée-size portions. You will be making the pasta as an appetizer for 270 guests. You figure that $\frac{1}{3}$ of an entrée-size portion will make one appetizer. What is the recipe conversion factor?

_____

_____

_____

_____

_____

Kitchen Ratios

Y ou are working in the kitchen of a café and need to make pie dough. You check the walk-in and discover that there are only 5 pounds of butter left. How much flour and liquid should you add to the butter to have the correct ratio for pie dough? The ratio for pie dough is:

3 parts flour
2 parts fat
1 part liquid

In this chapter the use of kitchen ratios such as this one will be discussed.

OBJECTIVES

- Calculate ingredient quantities for a given ratio when the total to be made is known.

- Calculate the quantities for the remaining ingredients in a given ratio when the quantity of one of the ingredients is known.

USING RATIOS

The use of ratios is an important part of food preparation. A ratio can be thought of as a mathematically formulated recipe. Recipes deal in specific measured amounts. On the other hand, ratios give a specific relation between the ingredients expressed in terms of equal parts.

The standard mirepoix ratio—two parts onion, one part carrot, one part celery—is shown here.

An example would be the ratio for vinaigrette: 3 parts oil, 1 part vinegar. If this ratio were 1 part to 1 part, you would use the same amounts of oil and vinegar. Since there are 3 parts of oil and 1 part of vinegar, there will be three times more oil in the vinaigrette than vinegar.

By contrast, here is a recipe for Cranberry Chutney:

1½ pounds fresh cranberries
8 dried figs
4 oz minced onion,
3 cups sugar
2 oranges
1 cup chopped pistachios,
1 teaspoon cayenne pepper
¾ cup golden raisins

In this recipe there are four different measurements used to describe the ingredient quantities: pounds, ounces, cups, and teaspoons. Unlike the vinaigrette ratio, the Cranberry Chutney recipe gives unrelated quantities.

Many recipes can be converted into ratios. Remembering key ratios instead of large and sometimes complicated recipes can help to simplify the job of the chef. The use of ratios allows a chef to recall a large number of recipes by remembering one basic relationship (the ratio), rather than memorizing each individual recipe; the recipe can then be customized by adding seasonings and other ingredients. Customizing recipes by adding different seasonings and flavorings to old ratios is one way to create unique new recipes.

A ratio is described in parts. The parts must be the same unit of measure. It is up to the individual using the ratio to determine what that unit of measure will be. For example, tablespoons or quarts can be used to make vinaigrette using the ratio below, and the resulting vinaigrettes will vary only in quantity. However, the units of measurement must be the same. Tablespoons cannot be used for one ingredient of the ratio and quarts for the other.

The ratios that will be discussed involve a single unit of measure. These ratios can be applied using weight measurements or volume measurements, depending on the ingredients.

Ratios are sometimes given as percents. When this is the case, the percents should be multiplied by the total quantity desired to determine the proper amount for each ingredient.

One basic ratio used in the kitchen is the ratio for mirepoix (see photo, page 223). Mirepoix is a combination of chopped aromatic vegetables used to flavor stocks, soups, braises, and stews.

COMMON KITCHEN RATIO

MIREPOIX

Ingredient	Percent	Ratio
Carrots	25%	1 part
Celery	25%	1 part
Onions	50%	2 parts

Ratios calculated in this chapter will be given in parts.

Other common kitchen ratios in standard and percent form:

COMMON KITCHEN RATIO

White Rice	or	**White Rice**
1 part rice		$33\frac{1}{3}$% rice
2 parts liquid		$66\frac{2}{3}$% liquid
Brown Rice	or	**Brown Rice**
1 part rice		28.5% rice
2.5 parts liquid		71.5% liquid
Vinaigrette	or	**Vinaigrette**
3 parts oil		75% oil
1 part vinegar		25% vinegar

The ratios listed above will work with weight measures or with volume measures. For example, to make rice, you could use 1 cup of rice and 2 cups of water. Or you could make rice with 1 pound of rice and 2 pounds (32 fluid ounces) of water. However, this is not universally true for ratios. The only reason the ratios listed above may be measured in volume or in weight is because the difference of the weight of each ingredient in a cup is negligible. See the sidebar below for some special cases in which the volume-to-weight differences are important.

Many chefs think of short recipes as ratios. For example:

Chicken Stock
Yield: 1 gallon

> 8 lb chicken bones
> 6 qt water
> 1 lb mirepoix
> 1 standard sachet d'épices

Although it is not wrong to think of this as a ratio, it is not the type of ratio being referred to when discussing the math used to calculate ingredient quantities from ratios. This type of ratio is better referred to as a *formula*. This formula is really a short recipe, because the ingredients do not have equal units of measure.

CALCULATING INGREDIENT QUANTITIES WITH RATIOS

There are two situations that may occur in dealing with kitchen ratios: The total amount to be made can be *known* or *unknown*. For instance, if you have a recipe that calls for 12 ounces of mirepoix, you know the total amount you need to make with the mirepoix ratio. On the other hand, if you had 12 ounces of onions and wanted to use them for mirepoix, then the total amount to be made is unknown, but you do know the amount of one of the ingredients.

SPECIAL-CASE RATIOS

The ratios listed below were formulated using weight measures and will work only if the ingredients are measured by weight. This is because the same volume measures of different ingredients will not have the same weight. For example, 1 cup of flour weighs 4 ounces, and 1 cup of liquid weighs 8 ounces.

PIE DOUGH	COOKIE DOUGH	ROUX
3 parts flour	1 part sugar	3 parts flour
2 parts fat	2 parts butter	2 parts fat
1 part liquid	3 parts flour	

WHEN THE TOTAL AMOUNT TO BE MADE IS KNOWN

There are four steps for determining ingredient quantities when you know the total amount that needs to be made.

STEP 1. Determine the total quantity to be made.

STEP 2. Find the total number of parts in the ratio.

STEP 3. Find the amount per part for this situation by dividing the total quantity to be made by the total number of parts.

STEP 4. Find the amount of each ingredient by multiplying each ingredient by the amount per part.

EXAMPLE:

You will be making 10 gallons of soup. For every 1 gallon of soup, you need 1 pound of mirepoix. How many pounds of each of the ingredients should be used in the mirepoix for this soup?

STEP 1. Determine the total quantity to be made.

If you were making 10 gallons of soup and needed 1 pound of mirepoix for each gallon of soup, you would need a total of 10 pounds of mirepoix (10×1 lb = 10 lb).

STEP 2. Find the total number of parts in the ratio.

Mirepoix
2 parts onions
1 part celery
+ 1 part carrots
  4 parts total

STEP 3. Find the amount per part for this situation by dividing the total quantity to be made by the total number of parts.

Determine the quantity (in this case the weight) of each part. To do this, divide the total weight (10 pounds) by the number of parts there are in the ratio. For mirepoix there are 4 parts, so divide 10 pounds by 4 parts (10 pounds ÷ 4 parts = 2.5 pounds). Each part in our ratio will weigh 2.5 pounds.

STEP 4. Find the amount of each ingredient by multiplying each ingredient by the amount per part.

The final step in this procedure is to take the weight or quantity in each part (the 2.5 pounds) and multiply that amount by the number of parts for a particular ingredient.

Onions	2 parts × 2.5 lb =	5 lb
Celery	1 part × 2.5 lb =	2.5 lb
Carrots	1 part × 2.5 lb =	2.5 lb
	Total =	10 lb

Finding the total is a good way to check your work.

WHEN THE TOTAL TO BE MADE IS UNKNOWN

Sometimes you do not know the total amount that you will be making. What you do know is the amount of one of the ingredients in the ratio. For instance, the introduction to this chapter presents a situation in which you know the amount of butter that you have but need to determine the amount of flour and liquid to add to it to make pie dough.

There are two steps for determining ingredient quantities when the total to be made is unknown.

STEP 1. Find the amount per part for this situation by dividing the amount that you know by the number of parts it represents.

STEP 2. Multiply the amount per part by the number of parts for each of the remaining ingredients.

EXAMPLE 1:

You are working in the kitchen of a café and need to make pie dough. You have 5 pounds of butter. How much flour and liquid should you add to the butter to have the correct ratio for pie dough (3 parts flour, 2 parts fat, 1 part liquid)?

STEP 1. Find the amount per part for this situation by dividing the amount that you know by the number of parts that it represents.

Divide the 5 pounds of butter (fat) by the number of parts the fat represents in the ratio.

Pie Dough
3 parts flour
2 parts fat
1 part liquid

5 pounds ÷ 2 = 2.5 pounds per part

STEP 2. Multiply the amount per part by the number of parts for each of the remaining ingredients.

> Flour = 3 × 2.5 = 7.5 pounds
> Fat = 5 pounds (given)
> Liquid = 1 × 2.5 = 2.5 pounds or 40 fluid ounces of liquid

According to the calculations, 7 pounds of flour and 2.5 pounds or 40 fluid ounces of liquid should be added to the 5 pounds of butter to make pie dough. The total amount of pie dough that will be made is 14.5 pounds.

EXAMPLE 2:

Your chef hands you 7 pounds of chopped onions and asks you to make mirepoix using those onions. How many pounds of celery and how many pounds of carrots should be added to the onions to make the mirepoix? How many pounds of mirepoix will there be in total?

STEP 1. Find the amount per part for this situation by dividing the amount that you know by the number of parts that it represents.

Divide the 7 pounds of onions by the number of parts the onions represent in the ratio for mirepoix.

> **WARNING**
> Be careful not to treat the 7 pounds of onions as the total amount of mirepoix. This is the amount of onions only!

Mirepoix Ratio
2 parts onions
1 part celery
1 part carrots

7 pounds ÷ 2 parts = 3.5 pounds per part

STEP 2. Multiply the amount per part by the number of parts for each of the remaining ingredients.

> Onions: 2 parts = 7 lb (given)
> Celery: 1 part × 3.5 lb = 3.5 lb
> Carrots: 1 part × 3.5 lb = 3.5 lb

According to the calculations, 3.5 pounds of celery and 3.5 pounds of carrots should be added to the 7 pounds of onions to make mirepoix. There will be 14 pounds of mirepoix in total.

CHAPTER REVIEW

Ratios can be used to simplify a number of basic recipes. New recipes can be built on the foundation of proven, basic ratios. Creative approaches in which you add different seasonings and flavorings to old ratios will create exciting recipes that are unique.

WHEN THE TOTAL AMOUNT TO BE MADE IS KNOWN

There are four steps for determining ingredient quantities when the total amount that needs to be made is known.

STEP 1. Determine the total quantity to be made.

STEP 2. Find the total number of parts in the ratio.

STEP 3. Find the amount per part for this situation by dividing the total quantity to be made by the total number of parts.

STEP 4. Find the amount of each ingredient by multiplying each ingredient by the amount per part.

WHEN THE TOTAL AMOUNT TO BE MADE IS UNKNOWN

There are two steps for determining ingredient quantities when the total to be made is unknown.

STEP 1. Find the amount per part for this situation by dividing the amount that you know by the number of parts it represents.

STEP 2. Multiply the amount per part by the number of parts for each of the remaining ingredients.

CHAPTER PRACTICE

Answers to odd-numbered questions may be found on page 251.
 Use the ratios on the previous pages for any ratios that you might need.

 1. You will be making Basalmic Viniagrette for a dinner party you are catering. You will need 1 quart of vinaigrette. How many fluid ounces of vinegar and oil will you need?

_____

_____

_____

_____

_____

2. You are going to serve vinaigrette to 165 people at a luncheon. Each person will be served 2 tablespoons of dressing on the side. How many liters of oil and how many liters of vinegar should you order to make the vinaigrette for this luncheon?

_____

_____

_____

_____

_____

3. You have 3 pounds 6 ounces of sugar. How many pounds of flour and butter will you need to make cookie dough? How many pounds of dough will you have?

_____

_____

_____

_____

_____

4. You will be serving 325 people brown rice. You know that 1 ounce of raw rice, when cooked, will produce 1 portion. How many pounds of rice and how many gallons of liquid will you need to make the brown rice for this function?

_____

_____

_____

_____

_____

5. You have 8 pounds 4 ounces of onions. You want to make mirepoix with the onions. How many pounds of carrots and how many pounds of celery must you use if you will be using all the onions?

_____

_____

_____

_____

_____

6. The standard ratio for Dauphine Potatoes is 1 part pâte à choux to 2 parts peeled chef potatoes. How many pounds of chef potatoes do you need to order if you want to produce one hundred fifty 4½-ounce portions and potatoes have an 85 percent yield?

_____

_____

_____

_____

_____

7. If you need to make two hundred forty 3-ounce tart shells, how many pounds of each ingredient do you need if you use the standard ratio for pie crust?

_____

_____

_____

_____

_____

8. A special dough ratio is as follows:
2½ parts flour
2 parts butter
1 part liquid

You have 3 pounds 12 ounces of flour. How many pounds of each of the other ingredients should you add to make this dough?

_____

_____

_____

_____

_____

9. There is a banquet for 280 people and you need prebaked pie shells for Toffee Caramel Mousse Pie. Using the standard ratio for pie crust, compute how many pounds of each ingredient you should use if 1 pie will serve 8 people and requires 10 ounces of pie dough.

_____

_____

_____

_____

_____

10. The basic ratio for custard is as follows:

    4 parts milk

    2 parts egg

    1 part sugar

You would like to make 45 servings of custard, 4 ounces each. How many ounces of each ingredient should you use?

_____

_____

_____

_____

_____

11. The vegetable served for a party of 300 will be a combination of sautéed yellow squash and zucchini. You are using a ratio of 2 parts zucchini to 1 part yellow squash and serving a 6-ounce portion to each guest. How many pounds of each must you purchase if the yield percent for zucchini is 85 percent and for yellow squash is 95 percent?

_____

_____

_____

_____

_____

12. A Bourbon Press is 1 part bourbon, 2 parts club soda, and 3 parts ginger ale. Fourteen people order this drink, so you have to make a gallon of it. How many quarts of each ingredient do you need to use to make the gallon?

_____

_____

_____

_____

_____

13. You will need 8 liters of basic vinaigrette dressing. How many liters of oil and vinegar should you use?

_____

_____

_____

_____

_____

14. The chef has asked you to prepare 1 ½ pounds of roux for tonight's service. How many ounces of flour and how many ounces of fat should you use?

_____

_____

_____

_____

15. A basic chocolate sauce is produced with 6 parts chocolate, 5 parts heavy cream, and 1 part butter. If you were to make a chocolate sauce using 18.75 ounces of heavy cream, how many ounces of chocolate would you have to use?

_____

_____

_____

_____

16. The special dessert tonight is Chocolate Tart with Chocolate Sauce. Each portion of this dessert will require 2 ounces of chocolate sauce. You need to make 60 portions. Using the ratio for Chocolate Sauce from Question 15, determine how many ounces of each ingredient you should use.

_____

_____

_____

_____

_____

17. Use this ratio to answer Questions 17A–C.

Linda and Julie's Special Fruit Salad Ratio
   4 parts diced watermelon
   3 parts sliced banana
   3½ parts diced cantaloupe
   2½ parts diced honeydew
   ¼ part shredded coconut

A. You would like to make enough to serve 40 people 4 ounces of fruit salad each. How many bananas will you need to order to make this delicious summer dessert?

_____

_____

_____

_____

_____

B. If you have 7 1/2 pounds of cleaned watermelon, how many pounds of honeydew will you need to order to make this fruit salad?

_____

_____

_____

_____

_____

C. If you would like to make 8 1/2 pounds of fruit salad, how much of each ingredient do you need to have cleaned?

_____

_____

_____

_____

_____

18. Use the following information to answer Questions 18A–B. You are making rice. You have 2,268 grams of uncooked rice.

A. How many cups of uncooked rice do you have if 1 cup of rice weighs 8 ounces?

_____

_____

_____

_____

_____

B. If the ratio of rice to stock is 1 part rice to 2 ½ parts stock, how many gallons of stock should you use?

_____

_____

_____

_____

_____

19. Use the following ratio to answer Questions 19A–B.

Winter Fruit Salad
   3 parts apples
   2 parts pears
   1½ parts oranges
   ½ part mixed dried fruit

A. You would like to make fifty-five 3-ounce portions of Winter Fruit Salad. How many pounds of each ingredient should you order? The yield percent for apples is 85 percent, for pears is 76 percent, and for oranges is 62 percent.

_____

_____

_____

_____

_____

B. If you have ordered 6 pounds of pears, how many pounds of apples should you order to make this Winter Fruit Salad?

_____

_____

_____

_____

_____

20. Use the following information to answer Questions 20A–B. You have been asked to make twenty 4-fluid ounce Kahlua Coconut Mudslides for a party you are catering.

Kahlua Coconut Mudslide
   ½ part Kahlua
   ½ part Irish Cream liqueur
   1 part vodka
   1 part heavy cream
   1 part cream of coconut

A. Using the following information, what is your cost per drink?

$21.49 per liter of Kahlua

$20.99 per liter of Irish Cream

$19.08 per liter of vodka

$2.00 per 32 fluid ounces of heavy cream

$0.99 per 14 fluid ounces of coconut milk

_____

_____

_____

_____

_____

_____

B. If you charge $8.50 per drink, what is your beverage cost percent?

_____

_____

_____

_____

_____

21. Use the following information to answer Questions 21A–B.

Polenta

1 part uncooked polenta
3 parts liquid

A. You have 3 cups of uncooked polenta. How many cups of liquid should you add?

_____

_____

_____

_____

_____

B. You will be using 1 quart of liquid. How many cups of uncooked polenta should you add?

_____

_____

_____

_____

_____

Formula Reference Review

THE PERCENT TRIANGLE

The following triangle is a tool used to find part, whole, or percent.

$$\frac{P}{W \times \%}$$

EPQ, APQ, AND YIELD PERCENT TRIANGLE

The following triangle is a tool used to find the as-purchased quantity, edible portion quantity, and yield percent. It is identical to the percent triangle introduced in Chapter 1 (page 12), although the terminology differs.

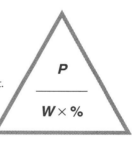

PART = Edible portion quantity (EPQ)

WHOLE = As-purchased quantity (APQ)

PERCENT = Yield percent (Y%)

$$\frac{EPQ}{APQ \times Y\%}$$

THE COST PER PORTION, SELLING PRICE, AND FOOD COST PERCENT TRIANGLE

The following triangle is a tool used to find the cost per portion, selling price, and food cost percent. It is identical to the percent triangle introduced in Chapter 1, page 12, although the terminology differs.

PART = Cost per portion

WHOLE = Selling price

PERCENT = Food cost percent

Cost
per
Portion

Selling
Price × Food
Cost %

THE COST PER BEVERAGE, SELLING PRICE, AND BEVERAGE COST PERCENT TRIANGLE

The following triangle is a tool used to find the cost per beverage, selling price, and beverage cost percent.

PART = Cost per beverage

WHOLE = Selling price

PERCENT = Beverage cost percent

Cost
per
Beverage

Selling
Price × Beverage
Cost %

For more information on beverage costing, please see Chapter 13, page 186.

CALCULATING THE AS-PURCHASED QUANTITY

$$\text{As-purchased quantity (APQ)} = \frac{\text{Edible portion quantity (EPQ)}}{\text{Yield percent (in decimal form)}}$$

CALCULATING THE EDIBLE PORTION QUANTITY

$$\text{Edible portion quantity (EPQ)} = \frac{\text{As-purchased}}{\text{quantity (APQ)}} \times \frac{\text{Yield percent}}{\text{(in decimal form)}}$$

DETERMINING COST PER UNIT

$$\text{Cost per unit} = \frac{\text{As-purchased cost}}{\text{Number of units}}$$

CALCULATING TOTAL COST

Total cost may be calculated using the following formula:

$$\text{Total cost} = \text{Number of units} \times \text{Cost per unit}$$

Must be the same unit

FORMULA FOR EDIBLE PORTION COST

$$\text{Edible portion cost (EPC)} = \frac{\text{As-purchased cost (APC)}}{\text{Yield percent (in decimal form)}}$$

DETERMINING FOOD COST PERCENT

The food cost percent is the percent of the selling price that pays for the ingredients. The formula for the food cost percent is:

$$\text{Food cost percent} = \frac{\text{Food cost}}{\text{Food sales}} \text{ or } \frac{\text{Cost per portion}}{\text{Selling price}}$$

DETERMINING SELLING PRICE

The cost per portion is used to calculate the selling price based on a desired food cost percent:

$$\text{Selling price} = \frac{\text{Cost per portion}}{\text{Food cost percent (in decimal form)}}$$

239

BEVERAGE COSTING

$$\text{Beverage cost percent} = \frac{\text{Beverage cost}}{\text{Beverage sales}}$$

CALCULATING THE RECIPE CONVERSION FACTOR

A recipe conversion factor (RCF) is a number that represents the relationship between the **N**ew and **O**ld recipe yields. There are three **NO**s of calculating RCF:

1. $\dfrac{\text{New recipe yield}}{\text{Old recipe yield}} = \dfrac{\text{N}}{\text{O}} = \text{Recipe Conversion Factor}$

   (Be careful not to invert this—you will get **ON** instead of **NO**.)

2. **NO** rounding of the recipe conversion factor.

3. **NO** units—the recipe conversion factor carries no unit.

Units of Measure and Equivalency Charts

B

COMMON FOOD-SERVICE MEASURES AND ABBREVIATIONS

Common Term	Abbreviation
teaspoon	t, tsp
tablespoon	T, tbsp
cup	C, c
pint	pt
quart	qt
gallon	G, gal
fluid ounce	fl oz
milliliter	mL
liter	L
ounce	oz
pound	lb, #
gram	g
kilogram	kg
each	ea
bunch	bu
to taste	tt

U.S. STANDARD WEIGHT EQUIVALENT

1 pound	= 16 ounces

METRIC PREFIXES

kilo- = 1,000 base units	
deka- = 10 base units	
deci- = 0.1 base unit	
centi- = 0.01 base unit	
milli- = 0.001 base unit	

Weight (Mass)	Volume (Liquid)
1 gram = 1,000 milligrams	1,000 milliliters = 1 liter
1,000 grams = 1 kilogram	

Weight Conversion between U.S. Standard Measure and Metric	Volume Conversion Between U.S. Standard Measure and Metric
1 ounce = 28.35 grams	1 liter = 33.8 fluid ounces
1 kilogram = 2.21 pounds	

VOLUME EQUIVALENTS

Volume Measures	Volume Equivalents
1 tablespoon	3 teaspoons
1 cup	16 tablespoons
1 pint	2 cups
1 quart	2 pints
1 gallon	4 quarts

ADDITIONAL VOLUME EQUIVALENTS

Volume Measure	Equivalent in Fluid Ounces
1 tablespoon	½ fluid ounce
1 cup	8 fluid ounces
1 pint	16 fluid ounces
1 quart	32 fluid ounces
1 gallon	128 fluid ounces

SCOOP EQUIVALENTS

Scoop Number	Fluid Ounces in One Scoop
4	8
5	6.4
6	5.33
8	4
10	3.2
12	2.66
16	2
20	1.6
24	1.33
30	1.06
40	0.8
60	0.53

Approximate Volume to Weight Chart

and Approximate Yield of Fruits and Vegetables Chart

APPROXIMATE VOLUME TO WEIGHT CHART

Ingredient	Volume	Ounces	Ingredient	Volume	Ounces
Allspice, ground	T	1/4	Chocolate		
Almonds, blanched	C	5 1/3	grated	C	4 1/2
Apples			melted	C	8
peeled, 1/2 in cubes	C	3 1/3	Cinnamon, ground	T	1/4
pie, canned	C	6	Citron, dried, chopped	C	6 1/2
sauce, canned	C	8	Cloves		
Apricots			ground	T	1/4
drained, canned	C	5 1/3	whole	C	3
halves, dried	C	4 1/2	Cocoa	C	4
Asparagus†	C	6 1/2	Coconut, shredded	C	2 1/2
Baking powder	T	1/2	Corn, fresh, kernels†	C	5 3/4
Bananas, diced	C	6 1/2	Corn flakes	C	1
Barley, raw	C	8	Cornmeal, raw	C	5 1/3
Beans			Corn syrup	C	12
baked	C	8	Cornstarch	C	4 1/2
green†	C	4 1/2	Cracker crumbs	C	3
kidney, dried	C	6	Cranberries		
kidney, cooked	C	6 3/4	raw	C	4
lima, cooked	C	8	sauce	C	8
lima, dried	C	6 1/2	Cream		
navy, dried	C	6 3/4	whipped	C	4
Bean sprouts	C	4	whipping	C	8
Beets, cooked, diced	C	6 1/2	Cream of tartar	T	1/3
Blueberries			Cream of wheat, raw	C	6
canned	C	6 1/2	Cucumbers, diced†	C	5 1/3
fresh†	C	7	Currants, dried	C	5 1/3
Bread crumbs			Curry powder	T	1/4
dried	C	4	Dates, pitted	C	6 1/5
soft	C	2	Eggs		
Brussels sprouts	C	4	dried, whites	C	3 1/4
Butter	C	8	dried, yolks	C	2 3/4
Cabbage, shredded†	C	4	fresh, whites (9)	C	8
Cake crumbs, soft	C	2 3/4	fresh, yolks (10)	C	8
Carrots, raw or cooked, diced	C	5 1/3	raw, shelled (5 eggs)	C	8
Celery, diced†	C	4	Farina, raw	C	5 1/3
Celery seed	T	1/4	Figs, dried, chopped	C	6 1/2
Cheese			Flour		
cottage or cream	C	8	all-purpose	C	4
grated, hard (e.g., parmesan)	C	4	bread, sifted	C	4
grated, medium (e.g., cheddar)	C	3	bread, unsifted	C	4 1/2
grated, soft (e.g., fresh goat)	C	4 3/4	cake or pastry, sifted	C	3 1/3
Cherries, glacéed	C	6 1/2	rye	C	2 3/4
Chicken, cooked, cubed	C	5 1/3	soy	C	3 1/4
Chili powder	T	1/4	whole wheat	C	4 1/4
Chili sauce	C	11 1/4	Gelatin, granulated	T	1/4

†Edible portion quantity

(continues)

APPROXIMATE VOLUME TO WEIGHT CHART (Continued)

Ingredient	Volume	Ounces	Ingredient	Volume	Ounces
Ginger, ground	T	$1/5$	Potato chips	C	1
Grapes			Potatoes, cooked, diced or mashed†	C	8
cut, seeded	C	$5^3/4$	Prunes, dried	C	$6^1/2$
whole†	C	4	Raisins	C	$5^1/3$
Ham, cooked, diced	C	$5^1/3$	Raisins, after cooking	C	7
Honey	C	12	Raspberries*	C	$4^3/4$
Horseradish	T	$1/2$	Rhubarb		
Jam	C	12	cooked	C	$6^1/2$
Jelly	C	$10^2/3$	raw, 1 in dice	C	4
Lard	C	8	Rice		
Lettuce, shredded	C	$2^1/4$	cooked	C	8
Margarine	C	8	uncooked	C	6.5
Marshmallows, large	80 ea	16	Rutabaga, cubed	C	$4^3/4$
Mayonnaise	C	8	Sage, ground	C	2
Milk			Salad dressing	C	8
condensed	C	$10^2/3$	Salmon, canned	C	8
evaporated	C	9	Salt	T	$2/3$
liquid	C	$8^1/2$	Sauerkraut	C	$5^1/3$
nonfat dry	T	$1/4$	Sesame seed	T	$1/3$
Mincemeat	C	8	Shallots, diced	T	$2/5$
Molasses	C	12	Shortening	C	7
Mustard			Soda, baking	T	$2/5$
dry, ground	C	$3^1/2$	Spinach, raw†	qt	$3^1/4$
prepared	T	$1/2$	Squash, Hubbard, cooked	C	8
seed	T	$2/5$	Strawberries†	C	7
Noodles, cooked	C	$5^1/3$	Sugar		
Nuts†	C	$4^1/2$	brown, lightly packed	C	$5^1/3$
Nutmeg, ground	T	$1/4$	brown, solidly packed	C	8
Oil, vegetable	C	8	granulated	C	8
Onions, chopped	C	$6^1/2$	powdered, sifted	C	$5^1/3$
Oysters, shucked	C	8	Tapioca, pearl	C	$5^3/4$
Paprika	T	$1/4$	Tea, loose-leaf	C	$2^2/3$
Parsley, coarsely chopped	C	1	Tomatoes		
Peaches, chopped	C	8	canned	C	8
Peanut butter	C	9	fresh, diced	C	7
Peanuts†	C	5	Tuna	C	8
Pears, fresh, diced†	C	$6^1/2$	Vanilla	T	$1/2$
Peas†	C	3.5	Vinegar	C	8
Pepper, ground	T	$1/4$	Walnuts, shelled	C	4
Peppers, green, chopped†	C	$5^1/3$	Water	C	8
Pimiento, chopped	C	$6^1/2$	Yeast		
Pineapple, crushed	C	8	compressed cake	ea	$3/5$
Poppy seed	C	5	envelope	ea	$1/4$

*As-purchased quantity

†Edible portion quantity

246

APPROXIMATE YIELD OF FRUITS AND VEGETABLES CHART

Approx. Wgt ea	Item	Yield %	Approx. Wgt ea	Item	Yield %
2 lb ea	Anise	75		Melons:	
	Apples	76		Cantaloupe	50
	Apricots	94		Casaba	50
	Artichokes	48		Crenshaw melon	50
	Asparagus	56		Honeydew, no rind	60
	Avocado	75		Watermelon, flesh	46
0.44 lb ea	Bananas	68		Mushrooms	97
	Beans, green or wax	88		Mustard greens	68
	Beans, lima, in shell	40		Nectarines	86
	Beet greens	56		Okra	78
	Beets, no tops	76	0.33 lb bunch	Onions, green (10–12)	60
	Beets, with tops	49		Onions, large	89
	Blackberries	92		Orange sections	70
	Blueberries	92	0.33 lb bunch	Parsley	76
1.5 lb bunch	Broccoli	61		Parsnips	85
	Brussels sprouts	74		Peaches	76
2.5 lb ea	Cabbage, green	79		Pears	78
	Cantaloupe, no rind	50		Peas, green, in the shell	38
	Carrots, no tops	82	0.33 lb ea	Peppers, green	82
	Carrots, with tops	60	0.19 lb ea	Peppers, fryers	85
2 lb head	Cauliflower	45		Persimmons	82
2 lb bunch	Celery	75	4 lb ea	Pineapple	52
	Celery root (celeriac)	75		Plums, pitted	85
	Chard	77		Pomegranates	54
26 oz ea	Coconut	53		Potatoes, red	81
	Collards	77		Potatoes, chef	85
0.58 lb ea	Cucumbers	95		Potatoes, sweet	80
1.25 lb ea	Eggplant	81		Radishes, with tops	63
	Endive, chicory, escarole	74		Radishes, no tops	85
	Figs	82		Raspberries	97
	Fruit for juice:			Rhubarb, no leaves	86
16 oz	Grapefruit	45*	3 lb ea	Rutabagas	85
3.5 oz	Lemon	45*		Salsify	63
2.2 oz	Lime	35*	0.03 lb ea	Shallots	89
6.6 oz	Orange, Fla.	50*		Spinach	74
0.125 lb ea	Garlic bulb (10–12 cloves)	87		Squash:	
	Grapefruit sections	47	0.83 lb ea	Acorn	78
	Grapes, seedless	94	1.8 lb ea	Butternut	52
	Kale	74		Hubbard	66
	Kohlrabi	55	0.36 lb ea	Yellow	95
0.75 lb bunch	Leeks	52	0.58 lb ea	Zucchini	95
2.25 lb head	Lettuce, iceberg	74		Strawberries	87
	Lettuce, leaf	67			

*The yield percent of producing juice.

247

Rounding

In culinary math, rounding is handled differently depending on the situation. The following chart summarizes all of the rounding rules covered in this text.

Solving word problems and determining ingredient costs on food cost forms	When solving word problems or determining ingredient costs on a food cost form using multiple steps, it is best *not* to round. However, you may leave your numbers truncated to the ten-thousandths place until you have arrived at your final answer. If you round drastically as you go, your solution will not be accurate.
Yield percent	As a rule, yield percent should be truncated at the whole percent to ensure that enough product is ordered to provide the necessary yield. So, 45.6% should be rounded to 45%, not 46%.
Cost per unit, total cost, and cost per portion	When calculating as-purchased cost, it is best not to round the number of units and the cost per unit. Rounding to the next higher cent should take place after the calculations are finished and the value for the as-purchased cost has been determined. Rounding in each step of the calculation may cause the answer to be significantly higher.
Recipe conversion factor	When calculating RCF, it is important not to round. This factor will be used to convert a recipe to produce a new yield. Once you have calculated your new ingredient quantities, you will have to round to more measurable amounts. Be careful not to round too drastically or the integrity of your recipe will be lost.
Amount to order	When calculating the amount to order, it is always better to round up. For instance, if you calculate that you need to order 45.3 pounds of potatoes, you should round up to at least 46 pounds.
Number of servings	When calculating the number of servings that can be obtained from a given quantity of a menu item, it is always better to round down and not count a partial serving as a whole serving. For example, if you calculate that you can obtain 16.7 three-ounce servings of green bean almondine from a recipe, it is best to predict that the recipe will yield 16 servings, not 17.
Selling price	As with cost per unit, selling price should be rounded up to the next higher cent. In fact, you may adjust this price to a more menu-like price. For example, $6.2345 would round to $6.25.

Blank Food Cost Form

For practice or for food costing, work use the blank food costing form on the following page, or use the interactive Excel food cost form at http://www.wiley.com/go/culinarymath for additional practice.

ELEMENTS ON A FOOD COST FORM

Menu Item: The name of the recipe identified as accurately as possible, using a menu number if necessary.

Date: The day, month, and year the cost was calculated. This can be important for later analysis.

Number of portions: The number of portions the recipe makes or yields

Size: The portion size normally served. This applies to menu items and is generally given in the recipe; it is not calculated.

Cost per portion: The cost of each serving. It is the total recipe cost divided by the number of portions.

FOOD COST FORM

Menu Item: _____   Date: _____

Number of Portions: _____   Size: _____

Cost per Portion: _____   Selling Price: _____   Food Cost %: _____

Ingredients	Recipe Quantity (EP)			Cost			Total Cost
	Weight	Volume	Count	APC/Unit	Yield %	EPC/Unit	
						TOTAL RECIPE COST	

Answer Section

Chapter 1

1. $\frac{5}{8}$
3. $6\frac{5}{12}$
5. $10\frac{7}{9}$
7. $\frac{3}{8}$
9. $\frac{5}{9}$
11. $7\frac{21}{32}$
13. $\frac{2}{7}$
15. $\frac{55}{268}$
17. Too many—answers will vary.
19. Too little—answers will vary.
21. Too little—answers will vary.
23. 1.5
25. 0.5
27. 0.4
29. 0.25
31. 5.2
33. 4.4
35. 75.4724
37. 5.7019
39. 2247.8386
41. 2.2825
43. 0.13
45. 72.85
47. 0.0025
49. 0.005
51. 1.25%
53. 0.001%
55. 112.5%
57. $\frac{9}{1000}$; 0.9%
59. $1\frac{23}{100}$; 123%
61. 0.875; 87.5%
63. Round down to 12; 0.675 is not a full serving.
65. Round up to $12.28; it is important to cover the partial penny.
67. Round up to 14; you cannot make a partial pie, so you have to make another whole one.
69. Round up to 6; if you round down, you will be short on watermelon.
71. 204 left over
73. 25 fluid ounces
75. 5.8% discount
77. 150 total staff
79. $558.24
81. 500 guests
83. 24% discount
85. 28% left over

Chapter 2

1. Weight is how heavy something is, and volume is how much space it takes up.
3. 8 ounces is weight, and 8 fluid ounces is volume.
5. A cup is a volume measure, and 9 ounces is a weight measure.
7. Answers will vary.
9. 0.8 ounces
11. 32 divided by 12
13. 3
15. 4
17. 16
19. $33\frac{1}{3}$% or 33.3333%
21. Gallon
23. 75%
25. $\frac{1}{4}$ cup
27. $\frac{1}{2}$
29. 16
31. No, parsley weighs far less than water does in a cup, so you need to weigh it.

Chapter 3

1. 33.8
3. 1 liter
5. 23.7%
7. 3 kilograms

9. Answers will vary.
11. 43.75%
13. 4
15. 5 cups
17. 0.1%
19. 33.8
21. 1,000
23. Sugar, kilogram; salt, gram; oil, milliliters; flour, grams; milk, milliliters

Chapter 4
1. 453.6 g
3. 0.1666 fl oz
5. $2\frac{2}{3}$ C
7. 14
9. 0.5
11. 4.75
13. 2
15. 2,500
17. 0.5859
19. 13
21. 64.52
23. 10.6666
25. 12
27. 32
29. 0.0625
31. 1.6406
33. 1.3227
35. 4
37. 0.6875
39. 0.3333
41. 0.0187
43. 12
45. 2.535
47. 11.2
49. 35.36
51. 1.701 kg
53. 2.5132#

Chapter 5
1. A. 2.5735
   B. 2.828

C. 3.7895
D. 3.2522
3. A. 15.1923
   B. 1.8934
   C. 3.7869
   D. 0.1183
5. A. 4
   B. 1.75
   C. 5.75
   D. 12.1875
7. A. 448
   B. 6
   C. 41
   D. 26.455
9. A. 3.25
   B. 0.7968
   C. 37
   D. 3.25
11. A. 3.4285
    B. 1.1808
    C. 4.5
    D. 6
13. 7.6875#
15. 88.28%
17. $5\frac{1}{3}$ T
19. 9 G 3 C
21. 60.41%
23. 40 portions
25. 3 kg
27. 50 oz or 3# 2 oz
29. 3 T
31. No
33. 2.6 C
35. 2.21 kg

Chapter 6
1. 1.3333#
3. 1.25#
5. 2.8125 oz
7. 3 boxes
9. 1.8#
11. 39 T
13. 76 T
15. 4 oz
17. $4\frac{1}{2}$#

19. 3.1875#
21. 123.0769 C
23. 3.6833 pt
25. 0.2343 oz
27. 9.7142 pt
29. 4.0625#
31. 30 T
33. 0.7291 oz
35. A. He assumed that molasses and water weigh the same.
    B. $\frac{1}{2}$ C or 4 fl oz

Chapter 7
1. Answers will vary.
3. 56%
5. 80%
7. 66%
9. 75%
11. 55%
13. 78%
15. Strawberries
17. 93%
19. 85%
21. A. A product cannot have more than 100% yield—75%.
    B. The yield percent is too low. There is not much to clean on mushrooms; 93%
    C. Very high yield percent—there is lots of trim on this fruit; 50%
23. 68%
25. 63%
27. 33%
29. 50%

Chapter 8
1. 18 heads
3. 21 anises
5. 12 breads

7. 92%; 5#

9. 86%; 8#

11. 85%; 10#

13. 52%; 5 each

15. 25 cakes

17. 72 servings

19. 3.5 oz

21. It is incorrect because you need to take into account the yield percent; 15 each

23. 74#

25. 75#

27. 7#

29. No, 5#

31. 6 pies

33. 2#

35. 32 each

37. 2 times

39. 34#

Chapter 9

1. $0.03 per fl oz

3. $4.20

5. $3.13

7. $0.24

9. $0.71

11. $0.27

13. $2.63/steak; 32 steaks

15. A. $3.99/jar

B. $0.50/oz

C. $0.11/tsp

D. $3.80

17. $7.95 is the better price.

19. $5.72

21. The 2-kg can is the better buy.

23. $0.72

25. $26.94

27. $0.50/qt; $0.02/fl oz; $0.13/cup

29. $8.82

31. $15.75

33. $1.46

35. $0.40

37. $0.24/ounces; $1.05

39. $0.11

41. 4 cases; $17.82 cost

43. $0.75

45. $1.20

Chapter 10

1. $0.71/#

3. $1.34/#

5. $0.42/#

7. $1.60

9. $0.93/#

11. $6.92

13. $15.27

15. $0.24

17. You have to pay for the waste; they are equal when a product has a 100% yield.

19. $2.67

21. $4.51

23. $0.62

25. $5.61

27. $6.55

29. $6.40

31. $0.05

Chapter 11

Food Cost Form 1

New Mexican Green Chili Stew

1. $0.20

2. $5.22

3. $3.75

4. $2.99

5. $0.05

6. $0.30

7. $0.14

8. $0.97

9. $0.60

10. $0.01

11. $0.19

Total cost: $14.42

Cost per portion: $1.442

Selling price: $5.77

Food Cost Form 3

Wilted Spinach Salad

1. $1.31

2. $0.13

3. $0.03

4. $0.17

5. $0.10

6. $0.23

7. $0.01

8. $0.03

9. $1.65

10. $0.26

11. $0.66

12. $0.09

13. $0.48

Total cost: $5.15

Cost per portion: $0.643

Selling price: $2.15

Food Cost Form 5

Angel Food Cake with Tropical Fruit Compote

1. $0.72

2. $0.16

3. $0.01

4. $2.08

5. $0.02

6. $0.13

7. $3.45

8. $0.73

9. $1.81

10. $1.26

11. $4.16

12. $0.16

Total recipe cost: $14.69

Cost per portion: $0.489

Selling price: $2.45

Chapter 12

1. 12#

3. 4#

5. 8#

7. 22 peppers

9. 4 pints; $0.43 per serving

11. No

13. No

253

15.

Food Cost Form

Eastern Mediterranean

Bread Salad

- A. $3.98
- B. $3.55
- C. $0.23
- D. $0.06
- E. $0.27
- F. $0.02
- G. $0.02
- H. $0.03
- I. $0.04
- J. $0.64
- K. $0.46
- L. $1.04
- M. $3.72
- N. $0.87
- O. $1.34

Total recipe cost: $16.27

Cost per portion: $1.627

Selling price: $5.43

Chapter 13

1. A. 12 cases
   B. $2.96
3. A. $1.02
   B. $6.17
5. 4 cases
7. 27 drinks
9. 65% poured; $8.21
11. $6.84
13. 973 drinks; 14.6%
15. 76 servings
17. 3 bottles

Chapter 14

1. 25.2 oz
3. A. 14.5833 tsp lemon zest; 29.1666 oz onion
   B. 2#
   C. 3#
5. A. 1.666666 RCF
   B. 1.875#
   C. 5 each
   D. $0.17
   E. 2#
7. 31.5 oz
9. 7.678 oz
11. 1.875 RCF
13. If you make the recipe in its original form, you are making 100 percent of it, and to find 100 percent of something, you multiply by 1; therefore, if you make more than 100 percent, you would multiply by a number greater than 1, and if you make less than 100 percent, you would multiply by a number less than 1.
15. The major benefit to using the recipe conversion factor is that it saves time and is easy to calculate.
17. 3.46 gal

19. 1.89 oz
21. 2.5 RCF
23. Answers will vary.
25. 13.020833 RCF

Chapter 15

1. Vinegar 8 fl oz; oil 24 fl oz
3. Flour 10.125#; butter 6.75#; total 20.25#
5. 4.125# each
7. Flour 22.5#; fat 15#; liquid 7.5#
9. Flour 10.937#; fat 7.2916#; liquid 3.6458#
11. Yellow squash 40#; zucchini 89#
13. Vinegar 2 L; oil 6 L
15. 22.5 oz
17. A. 8 ea
    B. 8#
    C. Watermelon 2.566#; banana 1.9245#; cantaloupe 2.2452#; honeydew 1.6037#; coconut 0.1603#
19. A. Apples 6#; pears 4#; oranges 4#; dried fruit 0.7366# or 0.75#
    B. 9#
21. A. 9 C
    B. 1 1/3 C

Culinary Math Glossary of Terms

AS-PURCHASED COST (APC): The cost paid to the supplier for a nonfabricated (uncleaned) ingredient.

AS-PURCHASED QUANTITY (APQ): The weight, volume, or count of a nonfabricated fruit or vegetable. In other words, it is the quantity (weight, volume, or count) of a product as it is received from the vendor.

BEVERAGE COST: The cost of the ingredients used to produce beverage sales.

BEVERAGE COST PERCENT: The percent of the selling price that pays for the beverage.

THE BRIDGE METHOD: The technique used to convert from one unit of measure to another.

BUSHEL: The largest unit of dry measure, equal to 4 pecks or 8 gallons.

BUTCHER'S YIELD TEST: This is very similar to the yield test for fruits and vegetables. The main difference is that the trim created during the fabrication of meat and poultry has value, whereas the trim created when fabricating fruits and vegetables generally does not.

CLEAN: The state of a product after it has been prepared to add to a recipe. This is called the edible portion quantity.

COST PER PORTION: The cost of each serving.

COST PER UNIT: The cost for one unit. The unit could be one of many things—1 peach, 1 ounce, 1 pound, 1 package, or 1 can.

COUNT: A term in the culinary world used to determine the number of a particular ingredient that is used in a recipe.

DECIMAL NUMBER: A number that uses a decimal point and place value to show values less than one.

DENOMINATOR: The "bottom" number in a fraction.

DIVIDEND: The number to be divided in a division problem.

DIVISOR: The number that the dividend is being divided by.

EDIBLE PORTION COST (EPC): The cost per unit of a fabricated (cleaned) fruit or vegetable. The EPC accounts not only for the cost of a fabricated product but also for the cost of the trim.

EDIBLE PORTION QUANTITY (EPQ): The weight, volume, or count of a fabricated fruit or vegetable. In other words, it is the quantity (weight, volume, or count) of a product after it has been cleaned, peeled, or prepared (fabricated) and is ready for use. The word *edible* in this term indicates that the product is ready for use in preparing a dish.

FABRICATED: The state of a product after it has been prepared to add to a recipe. See also *clean* and *edible portion quantity.*

FLUID OUNCE: A measure based on the amount of space filled by 1 ounce of water.

FOOD COST: The total cost of food items used in food production to produce food sales.

FOOD COST FORM: The form used in determining the cost of the ingredients in a given recipe.

FOOD COST PERCENT: The percent of the selling price that pays for the ingredients.

FRACTION: A number symbolic of the relationship between the part and the whole that has a numerator and a denominator.

GRADUATED MEASURING CUPS: Cups usually used for measuring liquids. They may be made of plastic, aluminum, or stainless steel. The common sizes are 1 cup, 1 pint, 1 quart, and 1 gallon.

HEAPING: A measure that is slightly fuller than level.

IMPROPER FRACTION: A fraction with a numerator that is greater than or equal to the denominator, such as $\frac{4}{3}$ or $\frac{4}{4}$.

KITCHEN RATIO: A relationship of ingredients stated in parts.

LADLES: Common sizes of ladles include 2 fluid ounces, 4 fluid ounces, and 8 fluid ounces. They are used for measuring liquid.

LOWEST-TERM FRACTION: The result of reducing a fraction so that the numerator and the denominator have no common factors. For example, the fraction $\frac{14}{28}$ reduces to $\frac{1}{2}$.

MEASURING SPOONS: Common sizes of measuring spoons are 1 tablespoon, 1 teaspoon, $\frac{1}{2}$ teaspoon, and $\frac{1}{4}$ teaspoon. They are used for measuring dry and liquid ingredients.

METRIC SYSTEM: The global language of measurement that has been adopted by almost every country. The metric system is a system based on the number 10.

MIREPOIX: A combination of chopped aromatic vegetables used to flavor stocks, soups, braises, and stews.

MIXED MEASURE: A measurement containing more than one unit. For example, 1 cup 2 tablespoons of flour or 3 pounds 2 ounces of potatoes are mixed measures.

MIXED NUMBER: A number that contains both a whole number and fraction, such as $4\frac{1}{2}$.

MULTIPLICAND AND MULTIPLIER: The numbers being multiplied.

NESTED MEASURING CUPS: Common sizes for nested measuring cups are 1 cup, $\frac{1}{2}$ cup, $\frac{1}{3}$ cup, and $\frac{1}{4}$ cup. They are used for measuring dry ingredients.

NEW FABRICATED COST AND NEW FABRICATED PRICE PER POUND: Terms used in a butcher's yield instead of edible portion cost. The new fabricated price per pound recognizes the value of the trim that resulted from the fabrication process. Unlike fruits and vegetables, the trim from meat and poultry has a greater value, which needs to be taken into account when calculating the new fabricated price per pound.

NONFABRICATED: The state of a product before it has been prepared to add to a recipe. See also *unclean* and *as-purchased quantity*.

NUMERATOR: The "top" number in a fraction.

PECK: A unit of volume equal to $\frac{1}{4}$ bushel or 2 gallons.

PERCENT: A ratio of a number to 100; the symbol for percent is %.

PORTION SCOOPS: Scoops that come in a wide array of sizes, which are numbered so that each number corresponds to the number of scoops it would take to make a quart. They are most commonly used to regulate single portions of finished food rather than ingredients.

PRODUCT: The answer to a multiplication problem.

PROPER FRACTION: A fraction in which the numerator is less than the denominator, such as $\frac{2}{5}$.

QUOTIENT: The answer to a division problem.

RATIO: A comparison of two numbers or the quotient of two numbers. A ratio can be expressed as a fraction, a division problem, or an expression, such as $\frac{3}{5}$, $3 \div 5$, or 3 to 5.

RECIPE CONVERSION FACTOR (RCF): A factor that is used to convert each recipe ingredient quantity so that the new recipe yields the new desired amount.

RECIPE COSTING: The process used to determine the cost of a given recipe.

RECIPE SIZE CONVERSION: The process of converting the yield of a recipe to produce a different, desired quantity.

RECIPE YIELD: The quantity a recipe produces.

REMAINDER: The number that remains after dividing.

REPEATING DECIMAL OR RECURRING DECIMAL: The result of converting a fraction to a decimal that repeats. If you convert $\frac{1}{3}$ to a decimal, the result is 0.3333333...(the 3 goes on infinitely). To record a repeating decimal, it is common to put a bar over the first set of repeating digits: $0.\overline{3}$.

SCANT: A measure that is slightly less full than level.

SELLING PRICE: The price paid by the customer.

TOTAL COST: The calculated cost of an item. In the food-service industry, it is important to remember that cost is based on how much of a product is used for a particular recipe, not on what is purchased.

TOURNÉ: A decorative knife cut used on vegetables that produces a football or barrel shape. It is considered one of the most demanding, time-consuming, and exacting cuts.

TRIM: The weight or volume of the waste. Trim, mathematically speaking, is the difference between APQ and EPQ.

TRUNCATE: To cut off a number at a given decimal place without regard to rounding (12.34567 truncated to the hundredths place is 12.34).

UNCLEAN: The state of a product before it has been prepared to add to a recipe—the as-purchased quantity.

257

VOLUME MEASUREMENT: As it applies to the kitchen, generally refers to the common measuring tools used in the United States, such as cups, teaspoons, and quarts. These tools are used to define the space that is filled with the products being measured.

WEIGHT: The heaviness of a substance. Weight is determined using a scale. In kitchens in the United States, there are two units of measure most commonly used to express weight: pounds and ounces.

WHOLE NUMBERS: The counting numbers and 0. The whole numbers are 0, 1, 2, 3, 4, 5, etc.

YIELD PERCENT: The percent of the as-purchased quantity that is edible.

Index

CULINARY MATH